ELDER
ROOTS and FRUITS

ELDER
ROOTS AND FRUITS

The Lives and Loves of a Formidable Family

ALLIE LOGIE

The people in this book are real. If I have offended or hurt any person or there are inaccuracies please forgive me. I'm only human.

FIRST EDITION

978-1-80541-286-1 (paperback)
978-1-80541-287-8 (eBook)

I want to thank my cousins
for contributing to this book
and to all who have given me support

Acknowledgements

I would like to thank my cousins for their contributions to this book. They will be sad that bits of the story will be missing and some bits not wholly accurate. I would like to have spent more time polishing it a bit but thought time is running out and the story must be told ! I would also like to thank my dear husband, Bill, for his support and for that of my children who are the most important part of my life.

I want to thank the publishers for helping me get this book off the ground.

If there are any profits from the book I would like them to go to the *Multiple Sclerosis Society* as three members of the Elder family suffer from this unkind disease.

Contents

Introduction

"I burst into tears when I heard the news of the Sinking of the Titanic," admitted my mother. She would have been 6 years old when she heard about the tragedy. This was one of the events that made the twentieth century such a turbulent time to live through. Many momentous events – the death of Queen Victoria, World War 1, the crazy Twenties, the Abdication of King Edward VIII and World War 11 were to have a great impact on those growing up during this time. The invention of the airplane, radio, television and the discovery of penicillin were also to make their mark. The following account tells the story of a family growing up in a Scottish manse from the beginning of the century to the end of it. It is told in a variety of forms – firstly, a straightforward telling of the Grandparents' stories, followed by the family's life in the Manse. The six children tell their own stories, growing up in Fife and Edinburgh and their subsequent careers. Gathering the material for this memoir, we find that the stories come in different forms. The eldest sibling, Hannah, an immigrant to Canada, was interviewed by her granddaughter, Millie, and has some insights into medical practice in this era. The second child was Hugh, known as Hugo, to distinguish him from his father, Hugh. He was the only boy in a household of girls and his story is told by his son, Hugh. The third, Jenny, who emigrated to Rhodesia (now Zimbabwe), told her story to her daughter, Catherine, and tells of her rapid romance and marriage in South

Africa. The fourth story is a collection of my own memories of my mother, the only one to stay in Scotland and who died earlier than her siblings. Next comes Dora who was the longest-lived and who died aged 103 and had plenty of time to pass on her story to her daughter, and lastly comes the youngest child, Pat. Her life is told by her husband and was the eulogy at her funeral. Hopefully, all these different lives and loves will bring together the essence of what it was like growing up in a manse and living in the turbulent 20th century and how it coloured and shaped their lives.

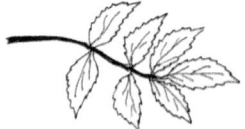

CHAPTER 1

Where It All Started – Grandfather, the Reverend Peter Macainsh

Rev. Peter Macainsh

Legend has it that one of the Macainshes was a schoolmaster in Monzie, a small village in Perthshire, and because of his alcohol problem, lived at the opposite end of the village from his wife, while the children ran between the two. We don't know if this man was Peter Macainsh's father, Donald, or a relative. Whoever he was, Peter must have been a clever boy (a lad o' pairts) as the local minister and schoolmaster took an interest in him and after he had served an apprenticeship as an ironmonger, he set off for Edinburgh at the age of twenty-five to study Divinity at the Free Church of Scotland's Hall of Divinity. How, one asks, could a young lad from a village afford the fees? Well, we think he was helped by his local Presbytery because we are told that he had been examined in Hebrew, Greek, Latin and

Theology to the entire satisfaction of the Presbytery. He could then proceed to his second year. It must have taken a great deal of hard work to complete the course. The big question now was what he should do next.

Lochgelly Church and Manse

We don't know why Peter opted for Lochgelly in Fife – perhaps he knew someone there. In 1855, this would have been a very different place to his home village of Monzie and to his student life in Edinburgh. Lochgelly owed its rapid rise and prosperity to the mining and iron industries which came when the railway extended from Dunfermline. So, it was a mining village of about 3,000 persons with a post office, library, two schools, a hotel and a police station. We have to remember that in those days, there was no Health Service, no social services – no welfare state. So the minister's role was one of counsellor, seeing to the sick and needy, and caring for the orphans and widows. Peter worked hard and he must have been popular as a church was set up in Lochgelly. After a year, he was ordained and the building of a church for 500 persons was started. You can see it in Lochgelly to this day – a fine church and substantial manse. (The Church in those days was the hub of social activity as there were few other diversions like now with sports, television,concerts, etc., to entertain people.) This says a great deal for Peter Macainsh. We are told he exercised a pro-found influence for good in the community. For years before retiring from active ministry, he engaged student assistants, paying their salaries from his own pocket. After sixteen years of putting his heart into the community, he found time at the age of forty-seven to find himself a wife, Hannah Brown Johnston, aged thirty-eight. We know little of this lady but presume she was local. They were blessed with one child, Hannah Gilbert.

Hannah Macainsh

In 1891, after serving in Lochgelly for 35 years, the Reverend Peter Macainsh retired to Crieff at the age of 67. There he built the substantial house of Knockearn where we all met for a family reunion. (This will be mentioned later.) How could a minister afford to build such a large place, you may be asking? Peter had inherited a large sum of money from a relation, Mrs Graham Gilbert (see

appendix for further information). Hannah Gilbert was the name given to the couple's only child. The inheritance allowed the family to live well and later to afford to pay for school fees for their grandchildren. Peter Macainsh lived the last few years of his life in the place he grew up, Perthshire, and died in 1913 in his eighty-ninth year. Hannah Brown nee Johnston, his wife, died in 1919 aged eighty-six having seen the outbreak and end of the First World War. They are both buried in the churchyard of Monzie beside the grave of his parents.

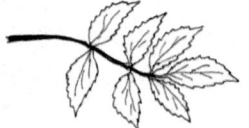

CHAPTER 2

Hannah Gilbert Finds a Husband

Hannah aged 9

So what did happen to the only child of the Rev Peter Macainsh and Hannah? We know she moved with her parents to Crieff when Rev Peter retired there. But what was a girl to do in the small town of Crieff – pleasant though it was? She possibly filled her time doing what Victorian girls did then – sewing, painting, making music, looking after her elderly parents. She had grown up in Lochgelly Manse. No doubt she helped her father and mother in running the parish and would learn the meaning of duty and service as well as learning about the Christian faith which was the firm basis of her whole life. However, at some point, she was sent to a good private school. We're not sure where it was or whether it was day or boarding. She was an intelligent girl, read widely and had many interests. Hannah must have been wondering what was to happen to her for, by the age of 26, she was still a spinster. This is where we get a bit of match-mak-

Elder-Macainsh wedding

ing. It was important for a girl to be introduced to a man in those days. No picking up someone in a bar. Just up the road from Knockearn House is the Hydro Hotel. Crieff owed a lot of its prosperity to its reputation as a Spa town. The coming of the railways had opened up the Highlands to new visitors, and so it happened that there was a young minister on holiday staying in Crieff Hydro.

For those of you who don't know Crieff Hydro, it is a large Victorian hotel, facing south, with a swimming pool, a solarium, fine restaurants and beautiful grounds and is a wonderful centre for family holidays even today. You may wonder how a minister could afford somewhere like the Hydro. Then, and even today, there were reduced rates for ministers of the Church of Scotland. It's possible that the Reverend Peter knew the Reverend Hugh from his Fife days as Hugh Elder was minister in the neighbouring town of Leven . Lochgelly, where the Rev Peter ministered, is only a few miles away. The Reverend Peter would have checked this young man out to make sure he was a suitable spouse for his only daughter. So what do we know of this intended groom?

Crieff Hydro today

Hugh was born in 1867 and was the fifth of six sons of Hugh Elder, farmer of Bearford Farm, Haddington (See family tree in appendix). After studying at Edinburgh University and the New College of the Church of Scotland, he served as assistant for the Minister of Galashiels and then was ordained in 1893 to the 'Charge' of Forman Church, Leven, Fife. This seems like a very suitable match for Hannah. One can only imagine Hannah's excitement at the prospect of meeting this very suitable candidate for her hand. Romance blossomed (you can imagine them wandering through the lovely gardens of the Hydro gazing at each other) and they were married in 1900. Hugh could not have found a more loyal and devoted partner in his life's work. Hannah moved to Leven and settled herself into the Manse which is described in the Ordnance Survey record of 1853-55 as 'a good dwelling house, two storeys high, having a garden and offices attached'.

Forman Church Leven

The Church is described as a plain building erected in 1843 at the end of Mitchell Street and seated to accommodate 750 persons. By today's standards, that was a big congregation.

CHAPTER 3

Hannah's Life in the Manse

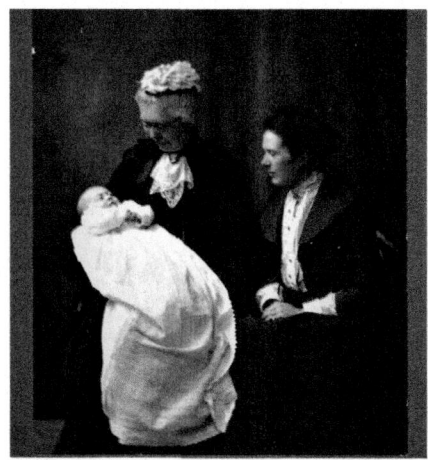

The three Hannahs, Macainsh, Elder and Robertson (nee Elder)

Hannah was to find her life very hectic, what with supporting her husband in his church work and also bringing up five children: Hannah was born in 1903, Hugh (Hugo) in 1905, Janet (Jenny) in 1906, Alison in 1907 and Dora in 1910. It took them three years to start a family and it was said that "Hugh only had to shake his pyjama trousers at her and another came along"! Jenny (second daughter) recalls her life in Leven – "Naturally, my memories of those years are very vague but I do remember that we had a swing on the lawn and that my father grew delicious strawberries in his garden. I also remember that Hannah and Hugo had a Governess, "Miss Whinnie", who came daily and I have been told that I insisted on sitting in on their lessons."

Educational oppor-tunities were not very good in Lochgelly so in order to provide a good education for the fami-ly, in 1910, they moved to Edinburgh where the Reverend Hugh became the Minister of Stock-

Inverleith Terrace today

bridge Church. As the manse provided was quite unsuited to a growing family, they bought a red stone semi-detached house in Inverleith Terrace (no 33) and added a third storey consisting of a big day nursery, a small bedroom and a large attic. Stockbridge was quite a deprived area in those days. This area, however, is one of the most expensive in Edinburgh now. At first, the family had nannies and then a "lady help" and most of the activities took place up in the day nursery. The night nursery was on the 2nd floor. It was later to become a bedroom for four of the girls while Hugo had a small room upstairs and Hannah had possession of the day nursery while she was studying medicine. It is interesting to note that ministers had staff to run their houses – cooks, cleaners, nannies. Wages were low compared to the salaries of ministers and other professional people.

When Dora was about two, a baby boy, Peter, was born but lived only two days, and in 1914, Patricia arrived. Hannah was sent to St George's School for Girls and Hugo to The Edinburgh Academy. Jenny and Alison, very close in age and who were usually treated as a pair and dressed alike, were sent to what can only be described

Hugh, Janet, Alison, Hannah Elder May 1909

as a Dame School which was within walking distance of the house. The School was run by two sisters, the Miss Givans, and consisted of two classes, one upstairs and one downstairs. The pupils used slates with slate pencils and sponges and a prize of a large poppy made of crepe paper was handed out at the end of each week. On their way to school, the girls had to pass the entrance to the Botanic Gardens and they used to stop and talk to the caretaker in his little hut.

Jenny writes, "I fear we must have often been late for school. I seem to remember a complaint from some older schoolgirls – possibly St George's – that two children had put out their tongues at them. We kept quiet!"

When Jenny was seven and Alison nearly six, they went to St George's which was then in Melville Street in adjoining houses. Their mother instructed Hannah, the oldest of the children, to look in on them at break and see how they were getting on but they didn't want to know her. Not long after Jenny and Alison had started at St George's, the school was moved to its new building in Murrayfield. This was quite a long way from home so they had to walk or cycle except when it was very wet when they were sent or fetched in a taxi.

School went smoothly for most of them. Hannah was intelligent and hard-working although not practical, Hugo showed promise at the Academy and Jenny was an all-rounder but her real interest was music and she proved a very competent

Hannah Elder and all 6 siblings

violin player. Alison was sporty, not interested in academia, but very musical and became an accomplished piano player. Dora was very conscientious, musical too and was a gifted cello player. Pat was bright and a bit of a rebel but the least musical of the lot. However, music did play a big part in their lives and the family presented a cup to be competed for by the houses within the school. It was known as the Elder Cup. They enjoyed singing in the excellent choir at school and, as there was no school orchestra, they played

Dora Elder 1928 St Georges School

in a small ensemble in the area. Music lessons were not taken at school but a teacher trained in theChassevant method came to the house once a week and took them in turns for lessons. At about nine, Jenny started violin lessons and was more successful at that than at the piano, though she and Alison did much duet-singing with that teacher. Hannah and Alison were the best pianists and gave up the violin and Dora became very keen and good on the cello. When it came to Pat, she learned piano under protest! It was thought that she felt there was quite enough music going on and she wanted to be different. She did her half-hour practice with a clock on the piano and stopped as soon as the time was up, no matter what place she had reached.

There was no tele-vision, and social media news information and topical event reporting were not as prolific as today but two things that made a big im-pression on the family were the sinking of the

St George's School 1928

Titanic and the outbreak of WW1 (more mention of that later). The family raised funds for the soldiers and their families and knitted gloves and socks for those on the Front Line.

During their school days and while they were at Edinburgh University and still living at home, they were much involved in the Church of which their father was Minister. Sunday was a busy day with morning service from 11 am till 12.30, followed by Sunday School in the Hall. In the afternoon, they were encouraged to go for a walk or else take it easy. Evening service was at 6.30 followed by Bible Class and, at times, they then took flowers from the Church to the sick. Hannah started a Primary Sunday School in which Jenny started teaching at the age of 15 and later, along with another girl, she took over from her as leader. In that way, she was, in a sense, prepared for dealing with numbers of children – a help when she had to take classes during her Teacher Training. Wednesday evenings were also devoted to the Church for they were members of the Girls' Auxiliary which met for an hour, and then they met with the other Primary Sunday School teachers to prepare for Sunday. From time to time, they took part in short plays at the Church and helped with entertainments at which they sang and played. On one occasion, the family provided the whole programme for a "Church Evening". Their string trio also played at the Mothers' Meeting and other occasions – Alison on piano, Dora on cello and Jenny on violin. Alison remembers playing the piano for the outside Mission which took place beside the Water of Leith in the middle of Stockbridge. She pulled her hat well down over her face so that none of her school friends would recognise her!

Stockbridge was a rough parish where many of the men drank their wages before the money got home to their families. In order to set an example, Hugh Elder gave up alcohol and banned it from the house. So, he had to go to a pub (out of the area) if he wanted a drink! He probably went near the University where his grand-

Stockbridge Church today

children were to drink decades later. I believe only sherry was kept in the house to give to visitors. This temperate life was to be an advantage later as Hugh Elder had five daughters to marry off and an alcohol-free wedding would have reduced the costs considerably! Though, if people wanted to buy their own, that was possible. Fond though they were of the five girls, their level of conversation could be a bit overwhelming for the two Hughs, so father and son often retreated to the former's study.

CHAPTER 4

Holidays and Hard Times

Pony and trap

Holidays were spent with their grandparents at Knockearn in Crieff. The family travelled there by train and were met by horse and cab as there were no cars in those days. At Knockearn, the children were welcomed by Grandfather and Granny Macainsh and also by two faithful retainers, Cicely and Kate. The children enjoyed roaming in the large grounds, from the orchard with pear, plum and apple trees to the Witches Rock at the foot of the garden. They played all sorts of games such as hide and seek and particularly enjoyed the wood with its little hut. For a special treat, a Wagonette was hired and they set off for the Sma' Glen where they made a fire, boiled up a kettle and made some tea, having collected fresh water and scones from a small cottage nearby. On wet days, games such as Ludo, Snakes and Ladders, and Happy Families were played. Ordinary playing cards were not allowed as they were associated with gambling, which was severely frowned upon by the Free Church. On Sundays, biblical Happy Families were played with Matthew, Mark, Luke and John, and Shadrach, Meshach, Abednego and Daniel. Prayers were said every day by the Reverend Peter and later by Reverend Hugh.

It was while she was on holiday in Crieff that Alison, aged about 11, became very ill with what turned out to be a burst appendix. She was in Crieff Cottage Hospital for the best part of the summer holidays and spent her time looking out of the window of her room which overlooked the morgue. She wrote interesting descriptions in letters to her mother of the various comings and goings in this part of the hospital! On the deaths of Grandfather Peter in 1913 and Grandmother Hannah in 1919, one presumes that the holidays to Crieff came to an end. Knockearn was probably sold and the proceeds would benefit the growing Elder family. However, a family reunion was held in Crieff in 1989.

Knockearn was not the only place where the family enjoyed holidays. The whole family packed up everything – bed linen, towels, crockery, food and sports equipment – and travelled to Arran with their retainers for the whole summer holiday. A house was taken at Blackwaterfoot and beach days and golf (in amongst the sheep) occupied the young. It sounded a very carefree holiday for those in their adolescent years. Memories of a horse-drawn wagon loaded to the gunwales trying to climb the hill over to the other side of Arran were recalled by members of the family. Reverend Hugh would join them for a week or two and worked on in the parish during the summer.

Hugh was to have four years in Stockbridge before he joined the YMCA as Chaplain in France in 1914 on the outbreak of WW1. In July 1917, he writes to his congregation from the Front lines, "*When the wagons and guns had been unhooked, the horses watered, tethered*

Rev Hugh Elder
as chaplain

and fed, the boys made straight for our Hut, hungry, thirsty, anxious for a smoke and glad of an opportunity of resting and writing home to their friends... They had been in action on and off since January and had had a very rough time." (see appendix). It must have been a traumatic time for Hugh Elder seeing sights that he would never forget and which may have contributed to his mental health breakdown later in life. Other events which affected him were the abdication of Edward V111 and the outbreak of World War 2. Like most of the men of that time, he would never talk about it. He was a well-read man with a good sense of humour. His contribution to literature is a book called 'Respectable Sins' and a paperback book entitled "True Wellbeing Studies in the Beatitudes for Fellowship Groups and Bible Classes". Both can still be purchased online.

CHAPTER 5

Retirement and Grandchildren

Hugh and Hannah Elder served in Stockbridge till 1930 and moved then to the small town of Moffat in Dumfriesshire where he was minister at the Well Road Church until 1938. The Manse in Moffat became a meeting place for the young at times like Christmas when they would arrive from their places of work or study. It was here that Hugo brought a friend of his from Oxford, Eric Tucker. He fell in love with Dora and married her.

This ditty, written for Christmas Day 1937, gives us a flavour of their family life as they move to the next stage of taking life partners.

As Nineteen thirty seven nears its end.
Once more this pen takes up its thankless task
Of finding rhymes and metres, so to bend
Apollo's bow of verse. Your leave I ask
What time these humble couplets I present,
Unto you, ladies and you, so-called gents.

And once again beside the family fire –
(Those nearest feel the most of its grateful heat,

Those furthest off compelled to retire
Blow icy fingers in their cold retreat.)
The Elder family, though short of twain
Here celebrate their Christmas once again

With one addition. From his parents torn
Our Eric, though each day he sees his wife
Decides to leave his Oxford all forlorn
Remembering no doubt it was for life
He promised to obey, is close at hand
His Dora's willing servant to command.

What shall I say of Ireland's rocky port
Of Loaning Green, that model 'stablishment'?
Where sound at times the dishes thrown in sport
And wireless messages to Nowhere sent,
Where 'cello mingles music with piano
And Rufus revels gaily in guano.

This much at least is clear, that Marriage bonds
Do not appear to chafe, even though the cynic
May think Still   Life is better seen in ponds
And Mrs Edwin more at home in clinic.
The newly weds, though all line all to each,
Appal the stranger with endearing speech.

21

But we anticipate; for first should be
Account of Hannah's wedding in the rain,
Though not at Moffat. Much too learned he
Who could describe the rank and wealth and brain
(all medical), which thronged the Masons' hall,
Professor Johnstone dominating all.

Her husband's work detains her now at home.
(of course that sort of thing sounds rather well)
And Alison is not allowed to roam,
While Grant awaits with zeal the Leper's bell
And possibly, - who know?-that after dark
Revealing sores, will creep the odious Park.
That is of Moffat bringing nought but shame
Upon a noble and well honoured name

That soon will take our Jen, but do not sigh —oh
There's nothing much that can alarm us,
Considering Jack's other name is Chalmers.

Alas that Christmas nineteen thirty eight
Will see her far from hence on Affric's land,
Though she by then should have a pleasing mate
And negro servants up'n every hand.
Thus fate decides a family shall disperse.
Had no one married it would have been worse.
So soon will Moffat know this tribe not more,
Well Road a pastor it will surely miss.

In February then from England's shore
Will sail the parents, leading forth to bliss

(At least we hope so) yet another bride,
And Pat to do some flirting on the side.

For only she remains as yet to bless
Her parents' age, and rightly so, unbooked
For some time longer. Doubt not none the less
They would be pleased if she were safely hooked.
We fear that Hugo to accepted be
Will need th'inducement of a pound of tea.

There seems no more to say ; but we express
Our hopes for all throughout the coming time
In every way of joy and happiness,
And now th'exigencies of toilsome rhyme
Compel us to submit the Muse, I fear,
Will not emerge again before next year.
25/12/37   H.E E.J.G.T

In 1938, when Hugh Elder retired from Well Road Church in Moffat, he and Hannah settled in Colinton in the outskirts of Edinburgh. Sadly, they were to be separated in their retirement as Hugh took ill and was admitted to a mental hospital outside Edinburgh. He celebrated the Golden Jubilee of his ordination in 1943 and died seven years later at the age of 83. Grannie Elder lived on in Colinton until her death in 1954 aged eighty. Her house in

Grannie's garden

Grant Avenue in Colinton has very happy memories. It had a spacious garden, with a shed in which were exciting things like an ancient doll's pram, a furry rocking horse, children's bikes and a sandpit where her grandchildren spent many happy hours. The house, Ardkeen, became the home for her two daughters, Dora and Pat, whose husbands were away in the Second World War. They each had one child, Alison and Martyn. The house was run by an amazing housekeeper, Mary, who owned a little black and white dog, Scrappie. Mary had had a child out of wedlock and my grandmother gave her a job in times when illegitimacy was very frowned upon. Mary cooked beautiful meals and baked lovely goodies like melting moments with what ingredients there were due to rationing during and after the War. One of the favourite teatime treats was white bread covered in sugar, tinted pink by red food dye. There was a basement where we hid if a German bomber passed over. There was also an amazing linen cupboard halfway up the stairs where we would hide. Kept in this were the most beautiful china dolls with which we were allowed to play, very carefully. Other games at Grannie's were a puff billiards board and a bagatelle board. The board for puff billiards was circular with four 'holes' round the sides. Each player was given a puffer held in the hand and pumped furiously to propel a small cork ball across the board to the holes of the opponent. It could become a very fierce game; as could bagatelle. One of the other interesting contents in the house was a stereoscope. This is a device for viewing a stereoscopic pair of separate images depicting left-eye and right-eye views of the same scene as a single three-dimensional image. This was fascinating to us youngsters. Old-fashioned scenes would appear before our eyes.

Grannie Elder

One Christmas when we visited Granny, she had received a tape of the Canadian cousins singing "We will rock you". We were captivated by their Canadian accents. "We will rack you"! There was a wonderful warm feeling about Granny's house and we knew we were always welcome even when she became disabled with Parkinson's disease and glaucoma. These were not helped by her breaking her hip. I remember visiting her in hospital (the Elsie Inglis Hospital – a hospital for women founded by Elsie Inglis) her leg was in some sort of contraption with pulleys and ropes. At night, we prayed for her and sang her favourite hymn, "Now the day is over". My mother did a great deal for Granny and Grandad as she was the nearest offspring. Her siblings had made homes in Canada, Rhodesia (as it was then), Ireland, and England. I don't remember either of my grandparents' funerals. Children were not encouraged to go to funerals at this time. There is no doubt that our grandparents had a very profound influence on our parents' lives and subsequently on our lives.

CHAPTER 6

Offspring of Hugh and Hannah

Six Siblings – Hannah, Hugh, Jenny, Alison, Dora and Patricia

We have seen the beginnings of this family with Peter and Hannah Macainsh in Lochgelly in Fife and with Hannah and Hugh Elder in Leven and then Edinburgh and how the latter brought up their six children in the Manse. But what happened to these six offspring?

What careers did they follow, how did they meet their life partners, when did they marry and how many children did they produce, if any? In the next few chapters, I hope some of those questions will be answered. I'm allowing different members of the family to tell their own story – some recounted to daughters or granddaughters, then, in the case of my mother, I write what I remember of her. Some of the information will be repeated but will be told in the writer's own inimitable style

The world in which they grew up was very different to ours in the 21st century – no telephones, no electric light, no health service, no unemployment benefit, few cars and certainly very little air travel if any at all. The microchip was unknown as were all the different modes of communication. Contraception was basic and the responsibility was on the women to maintain moral standards. Having sex before marriage was frowned upon and girls who had babies out of wedlock (unmarried) were often cast out of the house. Gay people had a hard time as their relationships were illegal until 1967. I remember being told by an uncle that I (aged 17) should not know about 'these things'. In many ways, my aunts and uncle had a very privileged upbringing though they were never spoilt and were always expected to do something for the community and be aware of those who were less fortunate than themselves. They were brought up with strong ethical standards. They all married happily and their marriages endured a World War where partners were separated for years. Undoubtedly, having lived through many difficult experiences, the husbands and wives were not the same people who went away to war as they were when they came back. Fortunately, they all did come back. The relationships survived. All of them were lucky enough to have children and so the line goes on. Not a lot has been written about the spouses but as Sonny Sadinsky, one of the spouses called them, 'the Spice' in the marriage, and that is what they have been – bringing something new, unique and spicy into the family. They have been a wonderful source of support to their partners and it says a great deal about them that there have been no divorces among all six siblings. However, as somebody jokingly remarked, maybe they just didn't have the imagination and initiative!

So, we continue to look at the stories of all the siblings and we start with the eldest, Hannah the Doctor.

CHAPTER 7

The First Child – Hannah, the Doctor

Hannah was interviewed by her granddaughter, Millie Sadinsky, in 1990. The following is a lovely picture of Hannah Robertson as told to her granddaughter... (Unfortunately Page 13 has not survived.). This is how it was written out and I have left it as it was.

Just give me some, a like, almost statistics on your
birth. Where were you born, you were the first daughter.

My father was a minister in Eeeven, Fife in Scotaland and
that's where I was born and also where five out of the six
children were born. I was about seven, we moved to
Edinburgh, and that is where the boy that did not live
and your Aunt Pat was born. My father was a minister in
Edinburgh twoo, and we grew up in a house opposite ahe
Eritxnix botanic gardens.

What did your mother do, at your birth. We'll get into
your brothers and sisters and all that after.

Oh. They were married, I was born three years after they
were married. They were married in 1990, and as for what
my mother did: once you got married in these days you didn't
do anything and in any case, she never did have a
career. She lived with her parents as an only child, until
she married my father. I don't know of course what the
set up was in Fife because I was too young, but I do know
that in Edinburgh we had a cook and a house tablemadde and
a nanny xndxxx or a nurse/governess, depending on how old
the children were.

Is a nanny and a governess two different things?

Ya, if the children were very young it was a nanny; if they
were older it was a nursery governess. Life was so very
different from what it is now, that it is very difficult to
project back and you wonder what on earth my mother did with
all that help. As well as that there was a washerwoman came in
to do the washing every week, but remember there were coal
fires so wherever there were fires they had to be laid, the
ashes had to be taken away, the fire had to be laid with
coals and so on; there were no dishwashers or washers or
dryers and in the laundry – although it wasn't called a
laundery; it was called a washing house – there was a boiler
to boil the clothes to make them clean and the washerwoman
scrubbed them on a scrubber when required and hung them out
to dry, of course. And then that wo ld be one day, and then
the next day she would come back and do the ironing. And
there was no such thing as wrinkle-free material, synthetics.
There was either silk, cotton or wool and they had to be htvned.

Like you had so much help and all that; did a lot of families
have so much hired help or were you wealthy?

No, we were not wealthy. Ministers salaries were not high,
but my mother's father was able to give them an allowance.
I don't know how much of an allowance, but it was big enough
to allow this domestic help – although a lot of people did
have some and remember the wages they god were very low, they
got room and board but their wages were very low. I can't
remember how low they were but t ey were minimal, because
I suppose because of the extra money that wewere able to
have txxy due to your great grandfather,

What did he do?

cont. 2

① April 16, 1990.

Q:
OK, you had a lot of brothers and sisters, of course
A:
No, one brother
Q:
Oh: Did you spend most of your time with them or did you
have lots of other friends. Like were you really close
to your family

Oh yes, but, in a way, but I was the eldest and I can't
say that I - sure we had family times but I had a lot of
friends and I was at a school that played a lot of games
and I played lacross and I played tennis and I played
cricket so I had all sorts of friends through that

You had a governess?

When the young ones were too young to go to school we either
had a nurse or governess, yes.

So you weren't responsible for looking after the kids at all.

No, not really.

Did you have any special relationship with any of your si
sters in particular?

Well, I think Auntie Pat, the youngest one I had, prob be
cause I was that much older and we seemed to have the sam
kind of temperment and she stayed with me when she went t
university while I was in practice in Edinburgh.

What did she do in university.

Arts, she took an arts degree and then a secretarial
degree; she went to London and then when my parents with
Aunt Jenny out to South Africa when she was going to
marry Uncle Jack, Aunt Pat went with them.

Ok

That was in 1938

What do you remeber about St. Georges academically. I mean
I know it was good academically, but can you remember
any of your classes or your teachers? Did you have favor-
ite subjects?

You know, when you asked me about being friends with my
sisters, and our relationship, wehad fun amongst ourselves
I mean we played charades and all sorts of games like that
like we palled it cheyette and you called it croconole
(sp?) and did all kinds of games like that that we played,
and when we went away on summer holidays the whole family
went together and of course we swam and we played tennis
golf and things and we made frinds that way but we still
because of the size of the family we had a lot of associates
in the family to do things with.

Did you keep any friends from school that went on to
medical school?

Uh, four of us from the same school went into medicine.

So is that quite a bit?

... 2 (Apr 16/90)

Yes, but they werent my particular friends. My particular friends in medicine I made in medicine.

And that was Lily Dummer?

And I kept them oh afterwards for a long time but then coming over to Canada, the friendships deteriorated

Was Lily Dummer one?

No she was a medical friends, she wasn't a school friend.

But you met her in medical schol?

Well, I met her at medical school and after medical school we were together in a hospital.

Did you kept in touch with your medical school friends when you were in medical school or not really?

Well, one particular friend that I can remember that I kept in touch with, parob. two. They didn't live in Edinburgh so that if I wanted to see them I had to go out of Edionburgh. But I had a lot of friends.

Ok. Huh. What did you do with your friends. What were the things to do when you would be with your friends.

Well, things were slightly limited compared to what they would be today, but I supposed we went to the movies. Ther were a lot of still pictures (like slides?) yes, with speaking, but the movies had come in so we went and did that. As I say, sports came, we did a lot of that. I don't know what we did in the winter, but we learned to skate. And we'd go to the swimming pool together to swim. We'd go to skating rinks and skate. We'd might meet in eachothers homes and there'd be birthday parties organizated and we'd be invited to that.

So it was quite important that you'd be relatively athletic?

Yes, I would say so....at the sort of school we went to.

What about boyfriends? Did you have, like, because they wern't at your school, did you associate with boys just friends?

No notm really. You never asked boys to parties and at the school dances kxmx you danced with girls. Nxxhxyx You didn't have any boys.

No boys at all went?

No, no boys at all.

Were there girls who did go aro nd with boys or was that not at your school?

Oh, I suppose there must have been but you didn't really hear about it. Nobody boasted about it. It just wasn't done.It didnt ppen. Not in the kind of society I w s ... in with.

Ya, what about, were you ever exposed to, like, other society or were you quite excluded?

... 3 Apr. 16/90

If you mean did I have any contacts with grades? of society, well I had because my father was in a working class congregat ion so we were always in contact with them and we knew the kind of homes they lived in and we assoc with them while I wasin the choir at one time and another time I was I taught in the Sun School I was head of the prim dept of the Sun School and I trained the teachers who were certain-ly of another class background

So you weren't - I can't think of the word I'm thinking of - like shut off

No no not at all

What were your subjects like at school

We we had to have compul subjects to get into university. We had to have English, History; we had to have Latin, according to what we were going into, Chemistry and Physic Mathematics, Geography

What were the apssing grades, 50?

Oh, probably about 50 these days but much more than that to get into university

What was it

I reeally can't rmember. There were high awards, you had t to have so many higher subjects and so many lower, one of which was Latin. Did I mention French? We had to have lower Latin but the l.... had to be higher and I think they were mathematics, chem and phys as I was going on to Med, English, French and in History I imagine.

Do you remember any of your teachers? Were they all female ?

There was one I remember called Miss Crawfuld. She was called Pussy Crawford, I don't remember why, and she taught geography and funnily enough I had, after I came out to Canada, about many, maybe 15 years after I cam out I got a letter from her saying that somebody had come out who was very lonely and that the reason she was writing me was that she was a ffiend of her mother's and so I went up and you know who that was ... Joan McGrath (Really?) and I've known Joan all these years and it was because my teacher wrote to me (from the church, Joan McGrath).

There's a woman who's about MUM's age, maybe she's older, now is that Joan McG. She

She has children older. She's the one who does the platnum work and organizes the show down at the Olympic Harbor place. Well anyway. That's an example of a teacher knowing where I had gone. And Joan McGrath was at that time was living out at Amherstview....

Did you play golf?

Yes, I learned to play golf - used to sometimes go holidays. I didn't play golf when we went holidaying at Crieff, but if we didn't go holidays at Crieff we sometimes went to a place in Fife and I played golf there and for quite a number of years we had a house over on Aaron, and the routine was golf, tennis, swimming. The tennis courts and the golf course were together, and you met other people

you met other people who went there, and you met people
from other places and sometimes you kept up with some of
them fxora certain lenghth of time. I remember one girl
came out to Australia who I met, but I didn't keep up
with her for very long, married and went out to Australia.

You started to knit when you were quite young, didn't you?

... already asked?

Bridge and Reading.

Though I vaguely knew about bridge, I didn't really start
playing bridge until I came to Canada, until the60s with
when I took lessons with some of my friends, and then I
got invoved in duplicate bridge which I enjoy and I've
been playing ever since.

And your student told you yau you couldn't knit and watch
television at the same time. Why did you take students in?

I took my first student in the year you went to Quebec.
And one reason I took them in was I had room, and secondly
I thought that probably your mother would go to Quebec wit
an easier mind if I had somebody in the houss. It was
shortly after your grandfather died. And somebody told me
about a student (who?) She came from providence, Rhodes
Island (not Ritchei?) No, she was the 2nd. Then I wasn't
going to take another but somebody askedme to and she was
ax disaster (what?) I just didn't like her very much. I
think she liked me, but I didn't like her. I think the
trouble was too that she didn't – the other two knew how
to behave in a house and keep to the rules which I had, but
she rather tried to take a little vantage, x and I didn't
like that.

Ok, religion.

well, I suppose it's been my background because of a
grandfather who was a minister and then a father who
was a minister and it was represented to us, as a minister's family, that we had to show an example, and each
help father as was required with church things. And we
all did it, either sining in the choir or teaching in
the Sunday school, doing what was required of us. But
we had to show an example, and not stray from the manse
path in any way.

Did you, was it when you were younger was it a given
that you were to be relatively religious or was it sort
of pushed upon you, or did you feel any resentment?

Nobody every questioned it, it was just the thing that
we did; we were a minister's family and we had morning
prayers, we went to church twice on Sunday and Sunday
school – when we were that age – and there were certain
things on Sunday we weren't allowed to do. Forinstance,
we could not play cards on a Sunday, but we could play
writing games and you had a card game that was like the
Happy Families game only it had the names of biblical
characters on it (giggle, oh really?). We were allowed
to play that. Later on, I don't know how we amused

... 5 Apr 16/90

ourselves. I know in my grandmother's house we wouldn't
have been allowed to knit. I don't know whether you would
call that religion or not, but it was religious practice
and it was just a background and we didn't question whether
we (you?) believed in God or not, you just believed in
God because that was how you we e brought up.

Did you or any of your brothers or sisters ever turn
against all that, or feel resentment, or strongly...

No, I think it was so ingrained in us that if we did
anything out of l ne that would harm our father in his
work that nobody ever thought of it. Maybe we weren't
tempted too much, but I think we would have been
condemned by all the other members of the family if
anybody got out of line. I think probably it, I think
the oldest ones in the family probably towed the line
more as things eased up a bit as the younger ones went
into adulthood.

Did you follow religion when you left home?

I think I went to church, but not the way I did when I
was at home, certainly.

And did any of your sisters or brothers become very
fanatical?

No, no. We were very traditional. And I think, looking
back, that the you just didn't question things. You just
took for granted that that was that and perhaps it wasn't
very inquiring or intelligent but it would have hurt
your parents so much if anybody had rebelledor hadquestioned
anything that you just shut your mind to it and wouldn't
do it.

So were you close with your parents on a personal level?

Very close to mother. Not as close to father. No.
But you know coming from a big family had a lot of advan-
tages in that, you asked if they .... eachother and all
that kind of thing. As children, of course you did
because there were six of you. Certainly there was an
age span of 11 years. So you couldn't all play like
that as t ough you were the same age. And I suppose
the oldest being me helped with the youngst quite a
bit. But we had a garden at, where I was brought up in
Edinburgh and we kept rabbits in hutches. And that was
quite an interest. And we usually had dogs, a couple, and
they had to be walked and whatnot, and the rabbits had
to be cleaned and fed.

So now you keep in touch with all your sisters, by mail
and things.

Well we always had, and as Aunt Pat wrote in a letter
to me: thank goodness we are in the letter-writing
age group sowe still do keep in touch because we have
always been accustomed to write letters and now everybody

and everybody kust lifts the phone, but I got a lot of
mother's letters still now that she wrote to me when
I was in Canada and she was in Scotland, and mother never
got out to Canada.

Never? Did you got xxi back to Edinburgh often?

Well, I couldn't go back to start with because the war
was on and they had exit permits. So whenevee the exit
permit conditions came off, I started finding out
how I could get back because my mother had been ill -
she had broken her leg or something, - and so I wanted
to go back and see her. So I managed to get a flight
to Prestwick from I don't know, Montreal I suppose, but
it was in a converted Lancaster bomber and there were only
10 passengers. And we landed at Goose Bay and we got off
the plane and had a meal, and then we flew over to
Prestwick. And I came back the same way and I
don't remember how long I stayed. Probably about 2
weeks. Well, that was in 1946 and I waspreparing to do
this so I had a mother craft nurse, who had looked after
Bill, booked to come in and look after the children while
I went off so that was how I was able to do it. And then,
the next time I went over, weall went over to Oxford in 1950
where the Prof. of Obstetrics and Gynocology, Professor
Moir exchanged chairs with Daddy the same as they do
sabbatical now. This was a straight exchange. We moved
into their house; they movedinto our house and we were
there - your father was there for 6 months, from January
to June, and I stayed on - evidently the Moirs, we
didn't clash, for the children to finish school and then
we all went over to Ireland to stay with Uncle Eric and
Aunt Dora outside Belfast. And somebody made reference to
that at the reunion this time. Now the people who went
over: Auntie Pat went over with her three children, I was
there with my 3 children, Uncle Hugo and Aunt Mary were th
there with Hugh, Aunt Alison was there with her 3, and
of course Aunt Dora and Uncle Eric were there. And so
everybody was there except your grandfather and Grant
Peterkind. Your grandfather disappeared to Canada and
Grant Peterkin found some excuse for not going.

So was that the last reunion before this one?

Ya, that was 1950. And we were able to stay there because
Uncle Eric had a prep school and we stayed in the school.
Well that was 1950 I went over and in 1952 I went back bec
cause my mother was really quite ill. She had Parkinsons
and she was blind. And I went over, as a matter of fact,
when we were over in 1950 my father died. And in 1952 I
went back to see my mother and 2 years later she died.

How did your father die?

... 7, Apr. 16/90

Well, he had been ill for some time in a nursing home.
I don't. They never...diagnosed what he had, but when
I left for Canada he was also in a nursing home having
an operation for something or rather. They thought it
was probably some sepsis that was poisoning his mind.
I don't know what he had. You all went to see him, I
mean not you but your parents, Gillian...and he recog-
nised who they were. Otherwise he just wasn't with it
very much.

What did you do in Kingston, like when the family was
growing up? What did you do and things?

What did I do? Well, I suppose I kept house for one
thing. I was on vario s committees which I suppose gave
me some work. We did a great deal of entertaining,
especially after the war forinstance they had various
doctors' meetings and what not and the head of the
department was supposed to entertain the visiting
people. It seemed to me we were always having vistors
from Britain. As I say I was on various committees so
I'd have meetings about that. I was on Sunnyside, the
Victorian Order of Nurses. I was president of the hospital
auxiliary and pres. of the first women's committee of the
symphony. I did all kinds of things like that, and, I was
on the public health, the city of Kingston public
health department, whatever it was called (I've forgotten)
and anyway, I found myself quite well occupied with all
kinds of volunteer and social jobs. I also gave lectures
on first aid.

Tell me about the cottage.

Oh. Well, I think the beginning of the cottage was away
back. Our furniture came back out in awooden packing
case which wasput at the bakk of the garden. And the wife
of a prof at Queen's asked me if she could buy it, and I
said what for, and she said she wanted to have it taken
out and put on a piece ofproperty out at the lake
and she would use it as a bathing hut. So I said, well,
how about you having a loan of it as I might want it
as a play hut or something. So she, I suppose I consulted
your grandfather about this though it seems to me I did
most of the negotiating. Anyway. She got it carted
away. It was a big thing. And she put it out on apiece
of proeperty which is now very well developed, out at
Redendale now, right on the lake. Other people had cottagegs
out there. It is now Everest Point (I'm not familiar with
it). Well, anywya it has some grand houses on it now.
But in t ese days people had cottages. And she took this
packing case and put out ... it wasn't for a sleeping
cottage or anything. It was on a piece of bay wih
flat stones and you could dothis as a hut to undress in
and t en you could go swimming and thx I think she
kept cups and saucers and a propane stoeve. She had a
daughter and her frinds used to go out there. And so
that lasted for a few years and then her husband retired
and they decided to go back to England. So she said to

me that someone wanted to buy the hut. So I consulted
your grandfather and we decided, and I said ??didn't
want to sell it??? We were paying rent. She was paying
rent to the farmer. So we decided to pay the rent
instead and your grandfather wasn't very keen on the
thing, so I said to the McAskills, the Corrys and the
Macintoshes: Do you want to have this hut to go and
swim in whenever you like? Maybe not the McAskills, but
the Corrys and the Macintoshes. So we split the rent
and every now and then we'd go off there to swim with k
the kids. I mean more than everynow and again, but during
the summer. And this went on. And then your grandfather
said: that he would like to have something a little
better so that he could take the students out whenever
he wanted to. So he asked the farmer to put up
something a little better and he said yes. And then
a property in Reddendale itself came on the market
so your grandfather bought two lots right on the lakefront
at Reddendale and put up that hut that's now down on the
cottage. So we used to use it, you know the little bit
that's partitioned off as a kitchen. And I had cups
hanging up on hooks. And you could lift in a bit of the
counter and there was a bit of the sink there. And I
used to take the water out of the lake and wash the dishes
and whatnot. We had a propane stove right there to
boil a kettle. And we had an outhouse which is also still
down there – although nonone uses it now. And we used that
and we had fun. And a picnic table. And you could go
swim and you could undress in there and you could use the
picnic table to sit round, and prepare a small meal and
so on. And we used that for quite a number of years and
then we used to go down to the Davis' often and we used
to go out in Mr. Davis' boat. And on two occasions in
Mr. Davis' boat we saw this notice up For Sale on the point
and really without consulting me very much although he
did consult me a bit, your grandfather decided to buy
the property. And so that was what happened. And the one
stipulation that I had was a cottage with all ameneties.

What happened to the property at Reddendale?

We sold it.

And was it higher up on the market now?

Well of course now it's ridiculous how little we got
for it but we actually doubled the amount. I mean it was
something like 2,000 dollars a lot and we got 4,000
so we doubled the money which, and, you know you can't
complain about that.

No, and so then

And then we got the hut taken down over the ice of
something, I think it was hauled down, and the outhouse

was put up there anyway and I have never understood really why it wasn't kept up because when there are a lot of people down there there is no reason on earth why the men shouldn't go into the outhouse (Right, hmmm) but it's been allowed to overgrow. And we untertained a lot down at the cottage and it's been a great grief to me that the visitors book disappeared and we were broken into once and the on y thing that seemed to go missing was the visitors' book which just must have been someone throwing it away for mischief. I don't know. There may have been other things broken into too but I don't remember them. But the vistors' book was a record of all the time, of all the people down there, of all Gillian Elspeth and Bill's friends, all the rest of it, and at one time we were the only people who had a telephone, which of course we had to have because of your grandfather's work and the dock was like grand central station because all the kids would come in and use the telephone. But it was, we really had a lot of fun down there.

Who built the big cottage, and was there a sandy beach there already? What about thedock?

Yes there was a sandy beach there already but throughout the years more sand would be brought in, but the sandy beach was there, yes. At one time, somewhere, but it's got buried, was, is a chain or a some kind of iron something to hook a chain onto because the ferry went across at one time, so x you used to see it, but it's got buried through time, but it's somewhere there. It may be a bit of a chain (A cable?) ... a big iron thing. It wouldn't be, no it's not as big as, something to fasten something onto, an iron support of some kind.

Who built the dock?

Well, it's been built and rebuilt through the years. I don't know who built the dock. And we had at one time we had the back dredged - you know where the pont goes out and you can walk behind the storage hut right down t the water there. Well that was dredged out several times and there was another dock there, very sheltered and very nice and that was allowed to go. But I remember when Sally Williams Cooper were down there and Gillians's friends, they would go down and lie there because it was out of the wind, and the sun was, and that was where the boat was kept out of the wind and around the back.

So what sort of things did everyone do there?

Down there? Well no tennis court of cours. Badminton all the time. Sometimes we tried to play crocquet I suppose. Water skiing and boating and swimming and just the things you do now. Yes. And yo see the Davis' were across and the Davies' were down the river at that time, that was Michael and his friends, and then across the way on the Sandy Beach there used tobe a motel, and then some people bought it, and we were asked if we wanted a bit and we said, No, we had an allowance but I think now that was stupid because we'd have had a dock across the way and we'd have had a bit thre and you might have had that and the Robertsons the cottage.

Oh, yeah. What about other family holidays. Would you ever really do anything else during the summer?

Well, we went to Picton you know. For 3 years we had through the Carsons whom I don't see very much now, we went to Picton for a month and that was right on the sandy beach and that was a cottage. You see people don't rent a cottage with no facilities. A pump - you had had to pump the water. But it was great for the kids who were small at the time, I mean we weren't but the others were, it was 46,47,48 I think we were there - and you could just be put out onto the sand and you bu lt sand castles and you ran in and out of the shallow water There were 6 other families there and there were children you could associate with and nobody had boats at that time. You weren't worriedabout people going out too far or drowning and so on. And the reason we didn't go back was your aunt Ada, great aunt ada decided to come out and stay with us in 1949 and I just couldn't have taken Ada to a place like that. I mean it was shocking enough to me because I wasn't accustomed to all these non-water things, and here I couldn't possibly take Aunt Ada, your grandfather's sister. So I think at that time the White's took over the cottage for that month. (So that was your cottage?) No, no. We rented it. So the White's I think rented it from us at that time and they went out there for years, so by this time we couldn't have got it back. And so that was when we sent everybody to camp, to Camp Calumet. And that was the reason. If aunt Ada hadn't come out, we likely would have gone back to Picton although your father would say it was a bit far to go He came up for weekends. But I think we'd have gone back anyway because it was very good. Now it's all the outlet beach, now a national park.

Wasn't there a fire there?

Yes, I think when the Whites were there, but you could get the details from them.

And then your parents went to camp. Did all 3 go to the same camp? Yes. I didn't want to send Bill because he was still small. But if theycould go to the same camp as the girls - different sections but the same camp, I still think he was to small, but anyway he went. I don't know how many yearsthey wee there. And then in 50 we went to, they can't have gone in 50 because in 50 we went to Britain. They must have gone back. They were there in 1949 I know because that's the year Ada came out. Then in 50 we were in Britain. And what happened after that I'm not very sure. But I think we built the hut then because in about 1954 or 55 we had the cottage.

... 16, April (Page 11)

And we've had the cottage ever since

When you had the cottage you didn't goto Picton? (No) Picton was before the time you had the cottage. (Oh yes) So before you had the cottage you would go to Picton and Reddendale?

Well, we didn' stay in Reddendale.

That was daytrips?

Ya, oh ya. And I hadn't a car at that time so I had to be sure and get your grandfather's car. The cottage down at Howe Island started at about 54 or 55 I think it's 54, andI know that your mother and aunt Elspeth went to Camp Oconoto at one time and Bill went to Mazinaw

that was when they were older?

Ya, Bill wasn't so old, but once the cottage was there and your mother by this time

(change sides - something missed)

... always in Scotland, always there was some Scottish country dancing ... always an 8thsome reel, at least one, sometimes a 4thsome real, usually a Danxhing White Sergeant, and when I came out to Canada I thought the dances were so dull because xxxx didn't have because we didn't have any of that of course until we you did have some dances - I think at the first Symphony Ball they had highland dancing at it because.. were keen on that sort of thing. I'm not sure if it was the symphony or not, but anyway we did have a few dances that we did have a few dances t at we did do that in, Now I'd imagine that it would have changed b now but certainly up to the 40s it was regular.

You know what question I really want to ask you. Mum mentioned it but: Your hopes for your grandchildren.

Well, I would like them to be happy. I'd like them to find something that they would enjoy doing. I would like them to find a man or woman that they would love or marry and I would like to have some great grandchildren. So you'd better hurry up.

Well it might not be too far off.

Ellie told me I had to live to be 95.

Well, 3 or 4 or 5 years wouldn't be unreasonable for Ellie - I mean it would be sort of young but ...

Well, it was interesting you know, when I was trying to analyse some of the statistics for the reunion and we found that the 14 grandchildren had all got married and had stayed married - which in this day and age is quite a record - and then Sonny and I were going over any possible reason or any possible factor that might make that possible or probable and the only thing we could come up with was that nobody married very young. The youngest was about 25 or 26

Why do you think it is important to have one mate, which is, I guess, what you are suggesting?

One spouse? As opposed to half a dozen? Well, I think, I suppose it's the way I've been brought up But I thing you hope that the person you marry that you love them enough and they love you enough that you want to spend the rest of your lives together, and if you have

Apr. 16/90 ... 12

chiledren, I do think, I know children have become accustomed to broken homes but I still think thatto have a mother and father stay together is in.... for the children as long as it's a hp;§y household.

You have witnessed the faeminist revolution in a way. Do you think you have? You have seen as you said when they get married they stop work and now they don't.

You mean, what do I think? Well, now I sympathise. You have taken a lot of training and you've got interested in your subject and I think that it is now unfortunate if you have to give it up. But at the same time I think it is difficult, and not hnly for bringing up the children does it make it more difficult, but still the woman is doing most of the work, ádyou have to call it that; it's not a 50:50 business. You may say, okay, I'll get a nanny to look after the children and a cleaning woman to look after the house, but who takes the responsibility for engaging the nanny, for seeing that they're doing their job properly? Nearly always the woman.

So do you think the man should take over more, or do you think the woman ...?

No I think the man has to take over more something. If the woman 's career and the man's career are, say, of equal importance, then if it can be a 50:50 business, then the man should take more of the responsibility. And they're not doing that, most of them; a few maybe but not very many. And you read that everywhere. But I'm not far, I don't like the shooting feminists; I think they are aggressive. I think they are unpleasant. Maybe it's necessary to get equality but I don't t ink they take into account that physio-logically men and women are not the same and the women - if there are going to be any children at all - then it's the women that have to have the children. They have the nine months of carrying the baby; they have the discomfort; the pain and possible danger of labor and therefore to speak of equality is almost impossible because men and women are not the same. Of course the feminists would say I8m not saying they're the same; it's a case of equality. But it's very difficult to get equality between two things when they are not equal. Now, another thing that I'm against is the fact that they have to have so many women in a company or a partnership in a law office for instance like the arts school in Toronto that has said no men need apply for the next 10 years. I think people should be taken on their qualifications and on their ability, regardless if they are men or women, and I think it's difficult sometimes to hire a woman in the child-bearing age because probably she'll be off for maternity leave and that means a lack of contin-uity in the work she may be doing. Now, I'm talking about the higher educated positions where it's difficult for someone else to step in to do the work. So, I think the same about minorities. A person should be taken on their qualifications whether they are black, white, yellow or man or woman.

I agree.

But I'm old fashioned, and forinstance this fuss about the shieks and their headgear - my answer to that as it would be to anything

... 13

43

Apr. 16/90 ... 14

..... but the reason we can't is they won't want any extras down
there. They're going to have their own guests. Anyway, I just
figure: We'll deal with it and Bill's going to have a big party,
bigger than he thought.

Well, where else could they stay? I can take two, Milly says she's
coming to me, but probably maybe she wouldn't, and I suppose
that if we had one of these air mattresses somebody could sleep
in the den.

Thank you , mother. That may be ... swimming pool.

Or they could sleep two people in the guest room. As a matter of fact,
somebody .... could go in my bedroom, because the bedroom's big.

What do you think about abortion?

I think it is a very difficult question. I don't like it but I
think there are occasions when it is adviseable. I don't like the
people that say abortion on "demand" I know it's just a word
but somebody has got to do the abortion and by and large doctors
I think really don't like doing abortions. However, I think there
are occasions when they are necessary and therefore I am not
an anti-abortionist. I don't think they should be as a method of
birth control.

Right. What do you think about capital punishment. Last Question.

I think that's very difficult., because there have been instances
of people who have been killed when they were innocent, through
misplaced justice. I think on the whole I am against a life for
a life, but I understand the people who are not against because
there are certain crimes where you really think the committer of the
crime should not be left alive to possibly commit more. However,
I think on the whole I am against it.

abortion cont.
I didn't say if they said abortion on request it would be more appropriat—
Nana, are you keen environmentalist. In thiery, but I am not in
practice. Do you think it is worth it. Oh yes, I think of the
greening of the earth and the warming up is very serious, and I think
recycling should certainly be practiced because it is v ry
wasteful. Before I came out to Canada, in Edinburgh we recycled
newspapers. We bundled newspapers up and they were collected. Yes
we did, now whether that continued or not I don't know, but that
was in the late 30s.

Son: Wonder what they did with them. Prob. wrapped fish.

I don't know what they did with them.

Back to abortion: Mum: ispix speak to the ispix issue of how much
say men should have on the abortion question.

Well, a husband is one thing. A casual lover is another. But I
get furious when men get rabid about the abortion problem because
they're at this present time - goodness knows what will happen in
the future - they cannot bear children. Therefore they have no
experience of the discomfort and the pain and the danger that
the woman has. And therefore it is arrogant in the extreme to say
do not have an abortion.

Apr. 16/90 ... 15

But Mum, they're part of the human race, and what they are really talking about is the sensitivity, they might say, of people and the future - they would probably, the rabid ones, take the argument they're talking brave new world.

Well, this is all very well in theory, but in practice are you going to have, can you see a man taking, to start with he can't nurse the baby, they could put the baby in a ...., can you see that man, for instance, that Daigle case: Can you see him taking the baby from Day 1 and looking after the baby? Until he's prepared to do that he has no business.

He would say, that's beside the point.

It isn't. Somebody's got to look after the baby.

What if he said to the court: I will take the baby. I will look after it and I will do that.

Well, it would make his case stronger, but he's not to go through the pregnancy or labor.

So that he can't win?

No, I don't think so.

What about a woman and her own body and so on; that's essentially what you are saying? A woman has the right to determine what will happn to her own body. I don't think it is quite that simple. In other words, you are saying that women, we should not have to share the responsibility for bringing new children into the world.

If they are married, that's a different matter because, I suppose one could say, living together in a permanet (hopefully) relationship. Then they are undertaking to provide a home for that child together, and I think that's di different aspect. That is the family outlook on things but I suppose everybody doesn't agree with that.

I suppose you are saying on an individual case by case basis you're not going to say it is totally up to the woman to decide whether or not to have the baby, but generally speaking at least you are saying abortion should be available.

Oh yes, I've said that. But mind you I'll tell you what I don't like. I don't like, I don't like late abotions. I once had to a girl of 13 came - I don't know what the feeling about the abortion or anything else was in those days; I just don't think it was an issue. I know this case of a young girl of 13 who came into the mater hospital seven months pregnant and nobody knew who the father was. She'd been running around with the military or something, and a chief - a head doctor - said to me: Induce that girl and don't pay any attention to the baby. I mean, I just shudder to think nowadays of anthing like that happening.

So did you?

... 16

45

Apr 16/90 ... 16

Well, I was told to, I couldn't have refused. I suppose if I had been very conscientious about it I could have said, 'I'm not going to do it,' but it never would have occurred to me to do that. My chief said I had to do that and that was that.

It obviously seemed sensible to you.

Well, the girl was induced, the baby was born, and I said, 'Put that baby in an incubator.' I did not pay attention and say, 'Don't do anything about the baby.' He meant to leave it and let it die. Well, the baby did die, because the incubators in these days weren't up to the what they are now, but looking back: That was a terrible thing to do; it really was — to tell his resident not to pay any attention to the baby.

Well, at least he was consistent.

You could do these sorts of things. You knew that nobody was going to run out of the hospital and say, 'Do you know what doctor so-and-so did?' Doctors were godalmighty in these days.

I wonder if Dr. So-and-so would have induced a three-month pregnant: that wouldn't have been induction.

No, that wasn't. I suppose they were done but I just don't remember about it.

Was the mother in some kind of danger?

No, not at all. It was far more dangerous to induce her.

So it was simply a case of aborting,

Absolutely.

So did it give you nightmares somet imes?

Nope. It would give me nightmares now.

Did she know what was going to happen?

No, but her parents did. She must.

In November 1937, Hannah married Edwin Robertson. Hannah and Edwin were both studying Medicine at Edinburgh University at the same time. At one time, Edwin was Assistant Surgeon and Hannah was the Anaesthetist in the same operating theatre. The surgeon was reported to have said he had seen romances blossoming in

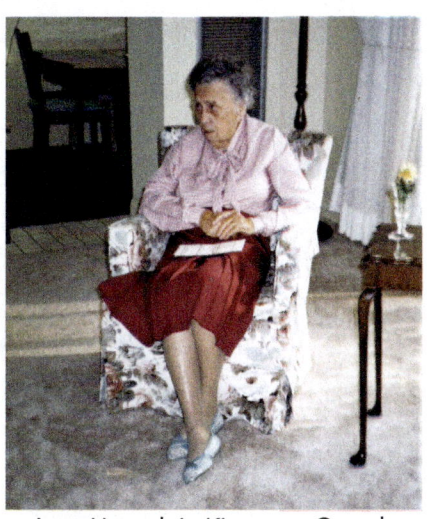

Aunt Hannah in Kingston, Canada

many places, but never before in an operating theatre! For many years, Edwin was the dark-haired man who first-footed the party at which Hannah was present. New Year after New Year passed and the family were surprised there was no engagement announcement. My mother remembers them being a very sentimental couple! It was learned later that Edwin didn't feel he could propose until he was earning a considerable income! Hannah and Edwin had three children – Gillian, Elspeth and Bill. Very sadly, Elspeth was killed in a car accident on her way back from work.

Alison writes:

I didn't know my Aunt Hannah well but met her on the occasions of the first family reunion in 1989 and on visits to Canada in 1987 and 1993. We visited her in her beautiful house on Great King Street (where Gillian and Sonny now live) and then in her condominium on Lake Ontario in Kingston. She came over

*as a strong, warm, highly intelligent old lady with a great in-
terest in all around her. She was a keen bridge player and, the
day after her death, her name was in the local paper as she had
won a bridge competition! She died at the great old age of 95.*

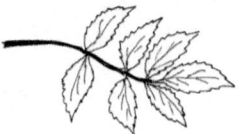

CHAPTER 8

The Second Child; The Only Son, Hugo, the Headmaster

My father, Hugh Elder, related by his son Hugh John Elder

Hugh Elder aged 12 – 1917

Daddy was born on 26 February 1905 in Leven where his father, after whom he was named, was minister of the Forman Church. He was the second of what were to be seven children: five sisters and another son Peter Macainsh who died as an infant and whom Daddy said he could hardly remember. Daddy was known as Hugo within the family to distinguish him from his father.

In 1910, the family moved to Edinburgh where my grandfather was appointed minister of a church in Stockbridge, now fashionable but then run down. The family home was 33 Inverleith Terrace, opposite the botanical gardens. Daddy was educated at Edinburgh Academy, from where he won a scholarship to Edinburgh University to read classics, in which he obtained a first-class degree. He had ambitions to read for the Bar, but in those days, although family money had paid for the children's education, it would not stretch to funding a young Advocate's training and early years of practice.

With five sisters at home, the house was a hive of activity. Daddy told me that if he wanted peace and quiet, he and his father would retreat to his father's study.

Daddy's next choice of career was teaching. Being advised that in order to make an impact he would need an Oxbridge degree, after graduating from Edinburgh, he secured a place at Corpus Christi College, Oxford where he spent two years reading 'Greats' (Greek and Roman history and literature and philosophy).

Daddy loved his time at Corpus and made many friends. One was Eric Tucker whom he took home to Moffat during a vacation where he met, and subsequently married, Aunt Dora. As well as studying, he took a full part in college life including playing rugby, a game for which he maintained a lifetime's interest, as he had earlier for Edinburgh Academicals.

Upon graduating with this second degree in 1929, he was appointed as an assistant master at Sherborne School in Dorset. I don't think he had ever been to the Southwest of England before, but he threw himself into all the extra-curricular activities that were expected of a young schoolmaster, including rugby coaching, the shooting eight, CCF and choral singing. He became a house tutor (deputy housemaster). He played the part of Pooh-Bah in The Mikado, which may be how his love of Gilbert and Sullivan originated. Some of his colleagues became lifelong friends and one was responsible for introducing him to my mother.

My father had rooms within the school precincts with a fine view of the Abbey. This was the first of several tied houses in which he lived; a perk, but also a trap for the very changed housing market that had developed by the time he retired. Sherborne was then, and still is, a lovely small market town particularly known for a former Benedictine Abbey and monastery, some of the buildings of which form part of the school. It was such a pleasant environment that many young masters stayed at the school for their entire careers.

A family connection with Sherborne also began, as I was to be educated there and Daddy's younger granddaughter Hannah went to Sherborne Girls' School, where she met her future husband (also Hugh) who was at Sherborne School at the same time.

After six years at Sherborne, Daddy felt that it was time to move on in order to avoid getting stuck, a move also prompted by a run-in with the then headmaster on the subject of schoolmasters' pay!

In 1935, he returned to Edinburgh to teach at Fettes College. I know little of that period of his life except that he was elected a member of 'The Spec', The Speculative Society, a literary and debating society founded in the great age of the Scottish Enlightenment and numbering among its former members Sir Walter Scott and Robert Louis Stevenson. I have his handbound history of the society and details of papers he delivered. I remember Daddy telling me how much he enjoyed and valued his membership.

Daddy was ambitious to progress in the education world. In 1938, at the early age of thirty-three, he was appointed headmaster of Dean Close School Cheltenham, now a well-known boarding

school, but then less distinguished and, as he was to dis-
cover, in a somewhat parlous
financial state. He later found
out that he was far from the
governors' first choice for the
role; others turned it down due
to their concerns about its vi-
ability.

However, at that age, you
worry less about such mat-
ters and he drove south in the
Spring of that year to take up
the position, and the occupation of the large headmaster's

Hugh Elder aged 38 – 1943 Swanage

house, in a spirit of optimism. Leaving aside the issue of the school's
future, he faced two immediate problems. He only had a few sticks
of furniture for a large house and also, being then unmarried, he had
no wife to play the important, albeit unpaid, role of entertaining
parents, governors and other dignitaries which was then expected
of a public-school headmaster.

The family solved both problems – his mother advancing him
funds for furnishing the house to the style that was then expected, and his younger sister Patricia (Aunt Pat) giving up her life in
London to act as his secretary and chatelaine of the Headmaster's
House. I never knew whether Aunt Pat was 'volunteered' for this
role by the family or if she genuinely chose it. Either way, it was an
unselfish gesture that helped Daddy to ease his way into the rather

stratified Cheltenham society. Some of Aunt Pat's letters home to her parents have survived and include hilarious descriptions of her time there.

Towards the end of his first term, Daddy was invited by one of his Sherborne friends, Hughie Holmes, to join a summer house party in Ireland for a couple of weeks' fishing. Holmes invited other Sherborne friends and his cousin Rosalie who brought along a friend, Mary Stagg. She was the then twenty-year-old daughter of a colonel in the Royal Engineers who had recently retired from Calcutta, where he had been in charge of the Royal Mint, to Swanage, a small coastal Dorset town. The issue of the headmaster not having a wife was on the way to being resolved!

Back in Cheltenham, Daddy set about re-organising Dean Close, including introducing rugby football as the main winter

sport rather than football, not least as this would create a larger fixture list with other schools. But not long afterwards, he suffered a burst appendix and subsequently peritonitis and, for a time, his very survival was in doubt. A lengthy conva-

Hugo with Mary in a boat

lescence was prescribed. Where better than the coastal air of Swanage? Recovery was successful and my parents' engagement followed. They married on 21 December 1939.

If his sisters were initially surprised at Daddy's choice of wife, a comparatively under-educated daughter of the Raj (as was then the custom for girls from her background), they never showed it and the perhaps formidable task of marrying a man with five well-educated and articulate sisters was made easy. On the other hand, Mummy's

Hugo in the countryside with Mary, Pat and friends

younger brother John, who was still at school, found the prospect of his sister marrying a headmaster somewhat daunting!

By the Spring term of 1939, Daddy was able to resume his duties at Dean Close, but international events were dominating everyone's thoughts. It was clear that the Munich Agreement of the previous summer was, at best, a breathing space before the inevitable war with Nazi Germany. In January 1939, Daddy received a top-secret letter from a senior civil servant stating that, in the event of war, the Dean Close School buildings would be requisitioned for Government use and the school would have to find alternative accommodation.

For a school already in financial difficulties, this news came as an existential threat. In the event, Daddy did a deal with Monkton Combe School in Bath, about forty miles away, in which that school's premises were shared, with one school having lessons in the morning and games in the afternoon and vice versa for the other.

Despite the worsening situation in Europe, there was time for another Hughie Holmes Irish summer house party in 1939 with my parents, by then engaged, and Aunt Pat, who wrote an amusing account of the holiday called 'Apud Ape', joining the party.

The declaration of war in September 1939 led to the threatened evacuation of Dean Close to Bath (a considerable logistical issue as the entire school buildings had to be emptied, apart from the chapel which was turned into a store). Nine months later, the Government concluded that it would not, after all, need to occupy the Dean Close buildings and the school was able to return to Cheltenham. From there, under Daddy's guidance, the school narrowly avoided closure and began its recovery so that successors could develop it into the leading school that it is today.

One of the Dean Close personnel, however, had no need to return to Cheltenham. Aunt Pat had met Uncle Andrew (Hurst) who was on the Monkton Combe teaching staff and they were subsequently married in the Dean Close School chapel, with my mother, the youngest wife in the Headmasters' Conference schools, as bridesmaid. Uncle Andrew had by then joined up and their wedding photograph shows him in military uniform.

Whilst the war years were hardly comfortable for anyone living in Britain, they were of course easier compared with those who served in the armed forces, particularly overseas. Daddy had been in the Territorial Army in the 1930s and, being thirty-nine at the outbreak of war, he would normally have joined up. However, not only was he in a reserved occupation, a legacy of his illness was that he was also deemed medically unfit for service. Although there could be no criticism of the position in which he found himself, he always felt uncomfortable about not having served, especially when so many of those whom he had taught went on to lose their lives. His account of the time records that of the fifteen boys who played in the inaugural school rugby match against Monkton Combe, five were killed in action, one lost an eye and the captain was wounded and taken prisoner of war.

Merchant Taylors School

Despite all the difficulties, my parents loved their time at Dean Close; perhaps in some respects the most enjoyable period of their married life. But when the war was over and the school's future was assured, it was time to move on. In 1946, Daddy was appointed headmaster of Merchant Taylors' School (MTS), a predominantly day school founded in 1561 by the City livery company of that name. Originally in the City of London, it had moved in 1933 to purpose-built accommodation in the outer north London suburbs set in 250 acres of grounds. It had none of the financial restrictions that had so affected Dean Close.

A fourth tied house for Daddy, even larger than that at Dean Close, a situation to which Mummy was also accustomed having been brought up in The Mint House in Calcutta. Also, an enormous garden, largely untouched since 1933. Once more, Daddy set about re-organising aspects of the school, in particular the house system, more along boarding school lines and, despite being a classicist, improving the science side and making key staff appointments, which were by then easier with so many former schoolmasters having returned from the war.

Missing from the headmaster's house, however, was the patter of tiny feet, a situation which was happily resolved with my arrival in August 1948 and my brother, another Peter Macainsh Elder, in June 1951.

Tragically, Peter was diagnosed with Wilms' tumour, a cancer now usually curable, when he was three years old and he died aged five in September 1956. This had a devastating effect on our little family from which, understandably, none of us completely recovered. Daddy's strong Christian faith, as a son of the manse, was temporarily challenged and my mother, who was also mourning the recent loss of her father, did a superb job of keeping him on an even keel. The large house seemed eerily quiet again.

Aunt Pat (and Uncle Andrew), who now lived a few miles away at Amersham, came to the rescue once more. I was fortunate in being treated by the Hursts as one of them. My cousins Hugh (eighteen months older) and Patrick (nine months younger) were close to me in age. Martyn was a bit older, but we all saw a lot of each other and all three went to MTS, with their uncle as their headmaster; perhaps for them a mixed blessing!

Many years later, Daddy told me that he had tried to move away to another school for a fresh start and was interviewed for Rugby School. But, by then in his fifties, and still affected by Peter's death, his application was unsuccessful.

Family summer holidays which, with occasional visits to the Tuckers at Rockport, had previously been spent with my maternal grandparents at Swanage, now moved to Boat of Garten near the Cairngorms, thus enabling Daddy to renew his Scottish roots. There was also a James Braid golf course. Daddy was an enthusiastic, if not always skilful, golfer. Mummy, who had taken up the game later in life, had a lower handicap and was ladies' captain of Sandy Lodge, close by MTS. At either end of the holiday, we would sometimes also visit Crieff and the Monzie churchyard, where family graves were to be found, as well as Aunt Alison and Uncle Grant in Edinburgh.

Meanwhile, the important task of maintaining and developing the reputation of MTS absorbed Daddy's energies, especially into the 1960s when society was changing so much as to challenge the traditional values with which Mummy and Daddy had grown up. As the crashing sound of my record of The Beatles *Twist and Shout* thundered out of the family radiogram in the drawing room, close to Daddy's study, it was clear that the youth revolution had even reached the hallowed portals of the headmaster's house!

Probably by then, Daddy was seen by the boys and the staff, although not by the parents, as somewhat traditional and old-fashioned, a view for which he would certainly not have apologised! A pupil at the time, who later became a headmaster himself, certainly thought so. But in a recent article in the school magazine, that same pupil wrote: *"I was fortunate to see enough of Hugh Elder to appreciate his qualities; subsequently, after 25 years as a Headmaster, I now hold him in very high regard"*. https://www.mtsn.org.uk/Concordia/2018Winter/6-7/.

Sixty was the fixed retirement age. When that time came, in July 1965, the Merchant Taylors' Company appointed a new head of about the same age as Daddy had been when he went to Dean Close. The Company made Daddy a liveryman and they and the former parents gave him a warm and generous farewell.

Retirement presented its own challenges. I was still at school with another couple of years to go, with hopefully university and professional training of some kind to follow; the 'tied house' arrangement ended and pensions were not as generous as they were subsequently to become. Also, Daddy had an active mind and some form of intellectual activity was a 'must'.

Few employers wanted retired headmasters. One exception was the founding owner of Millfield School in the Somerset town of Street, who had spotted that former headmasters added value and gravitas, at a very reasonable cost, to a school then regarded as somewhat nouveau and unconventional. Daddy joined the staff to teach classics at various levels, especially Oxbridge entrance.

The teaching accommodation consisted of somewhat spartan Nissan huts, and it meant my father taking orders from the head of the department, a younger and less well-qualified woman (shock, horror!). But he swallowed his pride and got on with the job, not finally retiring until ten years later when he reached the age of seventy, by which time I had qualified as a solicitor and was 'off the payroll'.

There were also plus factors. Daddy enjoyed being free from administration and able to concentrate on his first intellectual love of the classics. Furthermore, he formed a congenial bond with the other retired headmasters at the school. From time to time, they would go for lunch to The Elms pub when they would agree about the school's shortcomings and how they would never themselves allow the prevalent behaviour if they were in charge, etc. I noticed that by now, Daddy was becoming visibly more relaxed about life without having to retain, as he saw it, the aura of being a headmaster.

Meanwhile, Mummy and Daddy had found a house to buy (the first they ever owned), Millbrook, in the picturesquely named village of Huish Episcopi near Langport, Somerset, about a half-hour's drive from Street. Brick-built at the same time as MTS, it seemed a familiar setting. There was yet another extensive garden for them to get stuck into.

They threw themselves into local life, joined the church and various local societies as well as Sherborne Golf Club, the nearest reasonable golf course, and my mother helped out delivering meals on wheels ('muck on a truck', as she called it). They quickly built up a new circle of friends as well as welcoming many visitors from their previous lives. I liked the house but was only there during the school holidays and university vacations and then on breaks from London, where I always worked. Meanwhile, I met my wife Helen through a Huish Episcopi connection, as she shared a house with the son of one of their church friends, so it was a good move from my point of view.

Not long after Daddy's final retirement in 1975, he was diagnosed with Parkinson's, which gradually restricted his activities although it was fairly well-controlled by medication. Mummy, as she always had done, assumed an even more supportive, caring role.

Eventually, three weeks short of his eighty-first birthday, Daddy quickly succumbed to an aneurism and died on Friday 5 February 1986. He had been in great form at a lunch party on the Wednesday and was only taken ill that night. He had been looking forward to a visit from Aunt Pat and Uncle Andrew the following weekend which would have coincided with the Calcutta Cup which they were to have watched on television. The Scottish team put on a magnificent display that year, as if in tribute, winning the match by a record margin.

Huish Episcopi church was packed for his memorial service, with a warm address from a Millfield colleague. John Steane, a former master from MTS, played the organ including a piece he had composed especially for the occasion, and a former pupil and BBC Radio 3 presenter Cormac Rigby, by then a catholic priest, read a Shakespeare speech that he had last recited at an MTS Speech Day, chosen by his headmaster. The President of The Old Decanains also attended.

Mummy remained in Millbrook for another couple of years before moving into a new bungalow in Langport. Sadly, she also developed Parkinson's and dementia and eventually moved into a residential home in Langport with a fine view of Huish Episcopi church where, in August 1998, we laid her to rest. Her headstone also commemorates Daddy and Peter.

The family was always extremely important to Daddy. He greatly admired his maternal grandfather, The Reverend Peter Macainsh, as well as his parents. I never met his father and have no recollection of meeting his mother. Despite, or perhaps because of, their respective geographical locations, Daddy and his five sisters remained close. Letters, written on the thin blue air mail paper of the time, were regularly exchanged. I remember helping my mother wrap Christmas parcels for overseas dispatch to my cousins, many of whom later became frequent visitors to the Headmaster's House and Millbrook.

I count myself fortunate to have been born into the family and I have tried to follow its values and ethos.

Allie writes: *I remember Uncle Hugo well. I used to visit him and his wife Mary at the Headmaster's House, Merchant Taylors' School. Uncle Hugo loved producing Gilbert and Sullivan operettas. I was lucky enough to be at his production of HMS Pinafore and thoroughly enjoyed it. I was always warmly welcomed there. He and Aunt Mary used to holiday in Scotland taking the overnight sleeper with the car on the train to Stirling. We had great pleasure in entertaining them for dinner before they boarded the train for their return to the south. When he was working, Uncle Hugo was always very much the headmaster. We were delighted to catch him out one time when he was visiting our family in Edinburgh when he started eating dinner before Grace was said! After he retired from the demanding job of Headmaster, he became much more relaxed and his great sense of humour was allowed to emerge*

CHAPTER 9

The Third Child, Second Daughter, Jenny the Teacher

Related by herself, encouraged by her daughter Catherine

We take up Jenny's story: "I left school at 18 having passed the Scottish Higher Certificate, the entrance exam needed for University. For some reason, however, my mother felt that I badly needed some domestic training (I certainly was pretty useless and not much interested in domesticity). We agreed that I should go to the Atholl Crescent School of Domestic Science and take a Housewife's Diploma but also have violin lessons and attend a Chamber Music class and I rather think I kept on with my piano lessons. I did not enjoy the Atholl Crescent part and I'm afraid I adopted a frivolous attitude toward it but the enjoyment I got from the music part made up for the rest.

In 1926, I went to Edinburgh University and studied for an M.A. (Ordinary) Degree for the next three years. As a graduate, I was to be excused the first year at the Froebel Institute and thus miss a Nature Study course, so I chose Zoology as one of my University subjects. Apart from that, I had a very free choice and went to

Jenny and Alison Elder on Cruise

lectures given by Professors with special reputations. I thoroughly enjoyed my years at University and graduated in June 1928. As I was still living at home, I kept up my music and church work. The subjects in which I graduated apart from Zoology were British History, Economic History, Philosophy, Moral Philosophy, Fine Art and Psychology.

In September 1928, I went to the Froebel Educational Institute in Roehampton, London, for my Teacher Training Course. I was in residence there and being one of the few graduates, I had a room to myself! It felt rather like going to boarding school especially as most of the students had gone straight from home and were younger. I went into 2nd year and was joined by other people who had done their first year at other centres. Naturally, we became a group and stayed that way in the third year having rooms in a small cottage in the grounds, which was a converted pigsty as far as I remember. Grove House was a beautiful English Mansion in beautiful grounds including a lake and wonderful cedar trees. A number of outbuildings had been converted for residence but rooms in the house were also used as bedrooms. The dining room, library and other common rooms were on the ground floor. My first room was in a converted stables building.

Looking back, I realise I didn't make the most of such beautiful surroundings and could have taken my work less seriously. But I was determined to get a 1st Class Teacher's Certificate to back up my Degree and, of course, there was a lot of preparation during teaching practices. I also had several friends in London who asked me out for weekends and I was always glad of a break.

Towards the end of our third year, we all joined an agency and started applying for jobs. I soon found that my degree tended to be a hindrance as it really wasn't necessary for K.G. (Kinder-

Winners of Fancy dress Mediterranean cruise sometime between 1932 and 35

garten) and Junior teaching and made me more expensive! I finally got two interviews at the same time because I could offer music in which I had specialised. I had to travel to Leeds for the first one and arranged to go from there to Birmingham where I would stay the night before returning to college. It turned out to be a traumatic experience! As soon as I entered Leeds Girls High School and met Dr Lowe, the head, I felt that was the place for me. I had to explain that I had undertaken to go to Birmingham so would like to know my position and Dr Lowe had to find out if she could take a graduate. The outcome was that I was offered the job and promised to let them know as soon as possible. How I wished I did not have to face another interview! What made the Leeds job more attractive was that I met one of the staff who had taught Dora and Pat at St

George's. She probably gave a good account of my background to Dr Lowe.

My experience in Birmingham would make quite a long story! In short, they felt I was the very person for the job as it was a semi-missionary college and I was a minister's daughter with Church work experience. It was all very embarrassing and I had to reveal that I had been offered the Leeds job and felt I should take it as my first one. Also, I may say, I felt the atmosphere at the College would get on top of me. I had no one to discuss it with but never regretted my decision though the College actually contacted me a year later about a second try!

I taught at Leeds Girls' High School for 6 years from 1930 – it turned out that that was the very year Jack came to Rhodesia and I just missed him. The school helped me find digs with a single lady in a very nice road and I had a bedroom and a sitting-room. I could either take a tram to school or walk, which I often did on the way home. My landlady was very pleasant but would have liked to have been more intimate with me and meals were apt to be too casual at times. I had the midday one at school at first but later, had to ask her for a hot one in the evenings as at one time, I got rather run down. [note: for 'intimate' read 'pally' – change in implications of the word these days! – CH]

I taught in the Junior part of the school which consisted of 4 classes and was in a separate building along with the K.G. classes. All the staff were very friendly and helpful. I was the youngest both in age and experience. I had to go over to the main school to take first Handwork and later Scripture. I didn't enjoy that much although I got to know more members of the staff. Weekends tended to be a bit lonely at first but Mary Hall and I used to take a bus to Ilkley and do some lovely walks on the moors, sometimes having tea out.

The school had an Orchestra which I joined and thus met Helen Melrose. She lived with her mother very near Ford House where I taught and, as I got to know them, I was often there. At our first meeting, she asked me if I liked Chamber Music and would I like to join a quartet in which she played viola. It was in this way that I met Barbara Ellison who was our cello. We found that our sisters had studied medicine at Edinburgh together and that Hannah had actually written to Dorothy about my going to Leeds.

The Ellison family asked me to dinner initially but they became like a second family to me during all my time in Leeds. I often went there on Sundays and even out to their weekend cottage. Jim Park was often there and he and Barbara became engaged and married during those 6 years.

Helen Melrose also advised me to join the XXV String orchestra which Jim was conducting with Barbara in the cello section and Helen in the viola. At that time, I played the violin only and joined the 2nd violins. I thoroughly enjoyed the rehearsals every week and the various outings when we gave recitals mainly in Churches.

After their marriage, Barbara and Jim came to live much nearer me and I was often at their house. They used to talk about Jack and the prospect of his coming home on leave and how well he and I would get on! Then young Jim was born and in my sixth year in Leeds, Jack came home on leave and we first met at an XXV rehearsal. During his leave, he and Jim shared the conducting of several concerts and, naturally, I was round at the house, but on one occasion, he was away with Jim who travelled for his firm and I was up at Moffat for the school holiday. I was also in the midst of finding a new job as I felt that 6 years was long enough in a first one and I was very career-minded. During that holiday, I was offered one at my old school, St George's, which would lead to student teacher training and went back to Leeds deciding to accept it. Jack told me later that that distinctly shook him!

We had very few opportunities for doing things on our own but we did have a day golfing at Wetherby and we went to a concert at Bradford and so exchanged addresses at Jim's christening just before he went back to Rhodesia. It was no wonder, therefore, that letter exchanges played such a part in leading to our engagement and the fact that I was no longer in Leeds and embarked on a new post in Edinburgh didn't make things easier. *[Uncle Jim took Mum to buy the engagement ring as Dad was in Rhodesia. They didn't meet again until just before the wedding in Cape Town! They were engaged by letter for 18 months. CH]*

None of my family had met Jack so Jim and Barbara visited us all, Jim declaring himself the Carbon Copy! My father was due to retire from the ministry so he, my mother and Pat decided to take the trip to Africa with me and be at the wedding and get to know Jack. There was a terrific packing up as they were leaving the Manse at Moffat and I was also bringing a lot of things with me. At that time, it was better to buy household linen, utensils, etc., in England.

I think about 6 – 8 packing cases came from Glasgow to Beira and arrived by train some months after we were married.

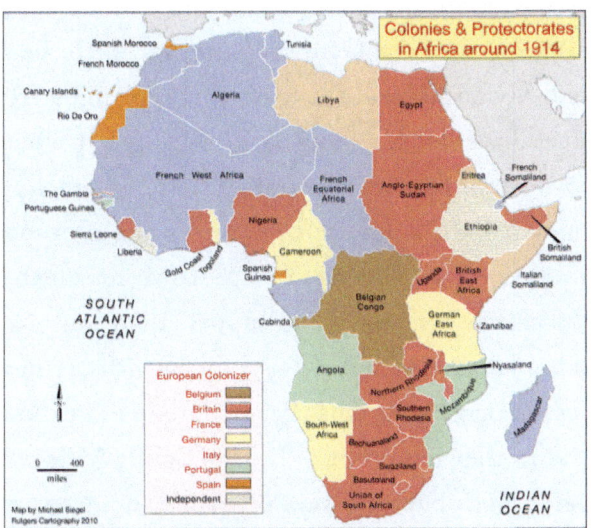

Map of Africa

We sailed on the City of Nagpur which was a one-class boat and took about a fortnight. Jack met us in Cape Town and we all stayed at the Gardens Hotel. We were married in the Gardens Presbyterian Church on March 1st 1938. Margaret Dick, a college friend, and her family rallied round and were a great help and several people we had met on the boat came to the wedding, but naturally, it was a small one. We had a delightful bonus, however, when Alban Hamer, a friend of Jack's from Leeds and organist at the Cape Town Anglican Cathedral, came and played for us and brought his choirboys to sing an Anthem. To have music like that just made the service. My father gave me away and then took part in the service and Pat was my bridesmaid. Jack had to get a business associate to be Best Man as unfortunately, he had no friends in Cape Town. [Mum said that when they were in the vestry to sign the register, she went down the passage to listen to the choir and had to be found in order to sign.] We had a Reception at the Gardens Hotel to which the choirboys were invited. My father read the telegrams explaining from whom they came, and we left for Hout Bay in Jack's car which he had brought down from Rhodesia by train. We were there for about 10 days during which the family came to see us one afternoon and we went on another day to friends in Cape Town for lunch and then up Table Mountain where we had supper. There was a small golf course at Hout Bay and we also went for long drives in a car lent by a business associate plus Chauffeur! Margaret Dick looked after the family until they left on their Tour of South Africa.

Jack and I came up to Bulawayo by train – an interesting journey for me through this strange country, and we lived for 4 months in a small house lent to Jack by a couple in his Choral Society. It was at the Hillside Road end of Grey Street and although I was almost eaten up by mosquitos from a pond in the garden, we were glad to have it as it gave us time to look round for a flat. My parents and Pat came to Bulawayo and stayed in the Palace Hotel and my father preached one evening at the Presby. Church in Abercorn St. He and my mother had a weekend in Salisbury where they stayed with Kennedy Grant who had been a young man in our Edinburgh Church. My father preached in his Salisbury Church. We did a trip out to Matopos and the family went to the Falls.

I have always been so thankful that Father, Mother and Pat came out to Africa with me. Not only were they able to meet and get to know Jack, but little did we know when they left that it would be nine years before we saw them again as war broke out the next year, 1939, and it wasn't till 1946 that we were able to get a passage to the U.K.

As Jack had already been in Bulawayo for 6 years, he already had many friends who called on me and asked me out. The Orchestra had had its first concert, Jack was President of the Music Club and Chairman of the Eisteddfod Society and naturally, I met people in connection with Philpott and Collins where he was Manager of Works. After the family left, we started looking round for a flat and found one in Princess Park Mansions at the corner of Selborne Avenue and Borrow St. It had one big living room with a kitchen off it, one large bedroom with a bathroom off it and it opened into a yard at the back. We found a factory which was selling furniture to the public at wholesale prices and it was there we bought our beds, a big wardrobe, the gate-legged table with chairs, the cabinet and a large bookcase. We found a 3-piece lounge suite in good condition in a Sales Room. Once we were in the flat, we had the thrill of unpacking the crates that had arrived from Beira with all the things I had brought out including linen, blankets, china, kitchenware and wedding presents. There was even a crate with a double bass from Jack's family home in 3 Belmont Grove, Leeds! I should explain that at that time, it was advisable to get as much as possible in Britain, I suppose because of scarcity and prices. We were lucky enough to find the Broadwood piano at a very reasonable price so it wasn't long before we had Chamber music evenings going. Jack already had a cello and I brought out a violin and viola.

Jack led a very busy life. His working hours were from 8 am – 5 pm but, as he was Manager of Works, he often had to go back in the evenings to supervise over-time. He also had rehearsals for both Orchestra and Choral Society every week and meetings in connection with the activities I have already mentioned. I soon transferred from the violin section of the Orchestra to the violas as there were so few of these.

After having led such a full life as a teacher, I found the days, and often the evenings, very long but as I was expecting Catherine, I had no intention of finding a job. She was born on Dec 19th 1938 at the Lady Rodwell Maternity Home. Life in the flat wasn't very easy with a small baby but we were lucky to live near the park where I took the pram every afternoon and we usually went out during the weekends. I was lucky in that the Sluces, great friends of Jack's and who had a baby a little older than Catherine, lived within walking distance, and I made friends with Mary Shepherd-Smith and Nora Hambly during our weekly visits to the Margaret Rose Clinic in Borrow Street, where our baby girls were weighed and advice given. [Elizabeth (nee Shepherd-Smith) and I are close friends to this day, although she and her husband still live in Bulawayo. I try to see them in Joburg when they come down to see their two daughters and their grandchildren. I saw them quite recently in August.]

In 1940-41, we found a house to rent at 20 Peard Ave, North End and having a garden made all the difference. By this time, "Granny Connor" had become very much part of our lives as a babysitter. We first made contact with her when Catherine was about 3 weeks old! Jack used to pick her up on his way from town and, during the war, after we had moved to Peard Ave, she used to spend the night and return with him next morning to save petrol. Without her, I doubt if I could have kept on playing in the Orchestra as any substitutes we had when she couldn't come were unsatisfactory, except for Mrs Mayne who couldn't be regular. Mrs Connor was with us for

Bulowayo

many years and we were very fond of her. I used to visit her in the Bartley Block where she spent her last days.

On October 22nd 1941, John Chalmers Park was born in Sister Roux's Home in Fort Street. His death at 3 weeks was a great sadness but we had to realise that if he had lived, he could not have led a normal life and Catherine was a great comfort. I was helped by the fact that St Peter's Diocesan School for Girls needed a teacher for Std 1 and there was a delightful Nursery School attached to it. So, Catherine and I went to school together. I taught there for a year and a term and left because I was expecting Malcolm. He was born at the Lady Rodwell on Oct 13th 1943.

When we were married in 1938, we had intended to try to take leave to go "home" in about 3 years. However, the outbreak of war in 1939 prevented that and it was not until September 1946 that we managed to get accommodation on the *Nea Hellas*. It was not a very enjoyable journey as the ship was also carrying many soldiers and the noise from their deck penetrated to our cabin, especially in the early evenings when the children were going to sleep. They

Ship to Africa

were put with me in a cabin for 6, along with 3 ladies, none of them very understanding. Jack was with five other men on another deck. He used to come down in the mornings and rescue Catherine and Malcolm for some fresh air while I got myself dressed. The journey took 5 weeks as we had to follow the Eastern route through the Suez Canal and the heat was most trying. It didn't help when we were delayed at Port Said with a broken propeller and, at the same time, not allowed to use that extra week to visit the Pyramids and Sphinx! However, we eventually arrived at Glasgow and, after a long wait for part of our luggage, which actually didn't turn up till later, we took a train to Edinburgh and were met by Alison and Grant very late in the evening.

We divided our holiday between our different homes and re-lations, but most of my time was with Mother while Jack went to Leeds and helped Billy, his younger brother, who was very ill with cancer. We had Christmas in Leeds with Jim and Barbara and some time in Ireland with Dora and Eric and actually left Catherine there for a term to go to school with her cousin Alison. It was one of the coldest winters on record but Malcolm had a grand time in the snow with his cousin Martyn, aged 4, who was also staying in Colinton, Edinburgh with my mother.

Jack had to return to Rhodesia after 5 months and spent the last one in Leeds helping Jim clear up his old home after Billy's death in January. I stayed on for another 3 months as I knew my mother was failing and also I had to wait for berths on a ship for myself and the children. During that time, Pat, who was with us with Martyn, had her second son and was also staying with Mother, so we had quite a busy time.

Catherine came back from Ireland shortly before we left. This time we were all in a big cabin of mothers and children where, incidentally, Malcolm picked up measles which he developed after we got back to Bulawayo.

<u>Janet Isabel Park</u>

<u>Continuation of her story by Catherine</u>

On our return to Bulawayo in 1947 my mother returned to teaching and Malcolm and I went back to school. Dad continued to conduct the orchestra and mum continued to play viola.

The next big milestone was the building of our house in Hillside – 41 Weir Avenue – in 1950, which was a great thrill as we had been renting all that time. I was married from that house and my parents lived there for many years, later moving to a small semi-detached house a little nearer the centre of Bulawayo and eventually to a cottage in a retirement village called Garden Park.

1957 saw the 50th concert of the orchestra, Dad's retirement as musical director, and the next visit to the UK where I started at St Andrews University. All of us travelled by ship to Britain, where we had a new car delivered to the boat and where we visited all the relatives and toured parts of Scotland and England. We were all able to see St Andrews and meet the Warden of my residence as well. There was quite a family reunion at Rockport with Hursts and Tuckers and a great time was had by all.

Then Mum, Dad and Malcolm left me with Aunt Alison in Edinburgh to spend the time before St A opened and they went via Leeds where Dad's twin to London. They flew back to Rhodesia, but the plane came down every night and they stayed in a hotel, so it took 4 days for them to get home. Travel has certainly become easier since then!

My mother came over on her own for my graduation in 1961 and Dad came over the following year when I was in Cambridge and was able to attend our performance of the St Matthew Passion in Kings College Chapel. At that time Malcolm was at Capetown University.

I returned to Rhodesia in July 1962 by boat and started teaching in Bulawayo where I met Bryan on the staff of the school. We were married in 1966 with Allie Logie as my bridesmaid. My mother loved her grandchildren, born in 1970 and 1971, and was always happy to baby sit. We spent 7 years at a school in Plumtree on the border with Botswana from 1971 to 1978, during which time we were affected by the bush war- not a good experience. During that time too, Aunt Dora and Uncle Eric came out to Bulawayo to stay with my parents and they spent a day with us in Plumtree.

In 1978 we went back to Bulawayo and bought a house very close to Garden Park so we were able to see a lot of my parents. Both of us were teaching and in a couple of years Bryan became a headmaster but by then, of course, my mother had retired after having spent at least 25 years in the profession and at various schools in Bulawayo. She is so fondly remembered by many of her pupils.

In 1984, in the face of increasing difficulties after Mugabe became president, we reluctantly felt that, for the sake of our children's futures, we should emigrate to South Africa. It was a hard decision because we had to leave my parents behind. We settled in Howick, Natal, and my parents were able to visit us several times. Both our children attended Rhodes University after completing high school.

Catherine's Wedding

Allie writes: *Jenny was to visit the UK several times after that and Catherine came to St Andrews to study for an English degree. After this, she went to Cambridge to study for her PGTC (Post Graduate Teaching Certificate). As it happened, I (her cousin) was there at the same time preparing myself to teach Religious Education. (Not a granddaughter of the Manse for nothing!) Jenny's last visit was in 1989 for the Family Reunion at Crieff. Having cared for Jack in the last years of his life, his death at the age of 90 gave Jenny the freedom to join the family at Crieff. I was lucky enough to visit the Parks in Bulawayo in Rhodesia (now Zimbabwe) in 1966. I was in Kenya on VSO and Catherine very kindly invited me to be her bridesmaid. It was just after UDI and I could not fly direct to Rhodesia then so I flew to Lusaka and then boarded a train to Bulawayo stopping at Victoria Falls on the way. It was a long and adventurous trip (that's another story) and I was so relieved to see Uncle Jack waiting for me on the platform in Bulawayo. Communications were poor then (not sure if letters got through, no mobile phones and ordinary phones not efficient) and he only guessed what train I would be on. I have some very happy memories of the time I spent with the Parks, the wedding, visits to the Matopos Hills, and outdoor cinemas to mention a few. I was given such a warm welcome. Aunt Jenny was also warm, intelligent and a great talker! Catherine and her husband, Brian, had to leave Zimbabwe because of the worsening security situation. It was hard for them as they had to leave everything. Aunt Jenny joined them later in South Africa and died there at the great age of 97.*

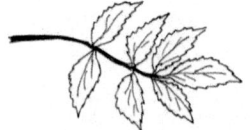

CHAPTER 10

The Fourth Child and Third Daughter, Alison the music teacher

As told by her second daughter, Alison (Allie)

Alison dressed as gypsy

Alison was the fourth child of Hugh and Hannah Elder. She was born on 1st December 1907 and grew up in the manse in Leven in Fife and in Stockbridge Manse in Edinburgh. She was very proud of her Fife roots. She was educated at St George's School for Girls as were the other girls in the family. She was not interested in academia but at school, she enjoyed games and music and indeed was a very talented musician. She passed her LRAM (Licentiate of the Royal Academy of Music). This is a professional diploma and is a licence to teach music. This she did. She gave private piano lessons around Edinburgh and even came to a house in Kings Park in Stirling. She also gave concerts and accompanied singers. She was very proud to declare that she was the first to earn her own living. This must have pleased her parents having 6 children to support through education. In 1930, when her parents moved to Moffat where her father was minister, we assume she moved into digs in Edinburgh. We know little of her at this point in her life. We do know that she went on a cruise with her sister Jenny and that they had fancy dress parties/socials. I'm sure she would still be helping at some church and playing music. Groups of young people would go to the Palais de Danse (which was a very upmarket dance hall in those days). Dinner dress would be worn and dancing would be to big bands. Some great music! One of mother's favourite tunes was "Spread a little happiness as you go by".

It was on one of those evenings that she met my father – a medical student. Grant Peterkin was the son of a GP in Forfar. At the age of 17, he had lost both his parents through illness and was living in digs in Edinburgh. He was attracted to my mother by her red dress and her black sparkling eyes. She had a gypsy look about her. She was a lovely looking young woman. At a later meeting at the Dance Hall, Grant remarked, "Thank goodness you're here. I don't

Grant and Alison just engaged

need to make polite conversation." They got engaged fairly soon but it was to be a long engagement. Mother thought when she met Grant she would be a GP's wife, but following an accident and a spell in hospital, he changed his mind and decided to specialise in Dermatology. This meant more training and more exams and eventually, they married in 1935. My mother said it was quite a strain being engaged for so long. People did not live or sleep together before marriage in those days so you can imagine tempers could get frayed.

Grant and Alison's wedding in 1935

Marriage in 1935 came as a welcome relief and with it came the end to mother's music career. Why? You might ask. As there was no Health Service in those days to make a living as a medical specialist, you would set up a private practice and also work in the public hospitals. If my mother continued working, it would look as though my father could not support her and therefore was not a good doctor. So, she became his receptionist, answering phone calls and showing people in. She found life at home rather boring then and I'm sure was a bit frustrated. Frustration also came from having three miscarriages. Eventually, after lying up for 6 months, she produced my sister Anne. Their joy was to be short-lived as war was looming on the horizon in Europe as Hitler flexed his muscles and invaded Austria and France. War was declared in 1939 and Dad was called up to the Royal Medical Corps. I was born during the Battle of Britain, July 1940, and our brother was born two years later, 1942, the year the Americans entered the War. Dad was posted to North Africa and Italy and served with the 1ˢᵗ Army. We must have missed our father as we dressed up an ashtray on a plinth and called it Daddy.

Meanwhile, Mother was left in a flat in in the centre of Edinburgh with three children under four. She decided to move to a house with a garden away from the city centre. Apparently, I was found climbing on the inside of the railings over a basement flat – a dangerous drop. This accelerated the decision to move.

Alison Peterkin
(nee Elder)

The move took us to a large stone Victorian house with an enclosed garden. It was here that mother contributed to the War effort by growing fruit trees and nurturing chickens which ended in the pot after supplying us with eggs. We had tremendous fun in the garden, climbing trees and walls, perching ourselves on roofs and cycling our bikes, treating some paths like racetracks. I broke a wrist crashing into a clothes pole! Mother gave us a great deal of freedom round the house and garden. Her life was, like that of many war wives, not easy. Bringing up three growing children was hard work and she had to use her initiative – making us clothes from old curtains, making a nightie out of her wedding dress, and feeding us with rationed meat, butter, eggs, and sugar. Eggs she collected from friends' farms and preserved them. We seemed to suffer from all the childhood illnesses – measles, mumps, whooping cough, scarlet fever – as well as other problems. (No vaccinations in those days) I had my tonsils removed on the kitchen table in one of our bedrooms where there was a basin. Later, I had my head sewn up having cracked it open on the edge of a gas mask. The Doctor came to the house and sterilised the needle on the kitchen stove. The first one snapped on my hard head and another had to be sterilised! Anne, my sister, was rushed to hospital with double mastoiditis. Most of the penicillin was directed to the War Front. After 6 weeks in a nursing home (no NHS in those days), she was discharged. It was tough as parents were not allowed to visit sick children in those days. Shortly after that, I was admitted to the same place to have my appendix removed after complaining of a sore stomach. Mother made sure I had the thing removed as she had nearly died of a burst appendix. Our brother had pneumonia at six weeks. So life was a bit of a roller coaster for Mother. It was during that stressful time that she took up smoking. We always blamed Hitler for her cancer and subsequent death as she continued smoking till she died. It was during this difficult time that an acquaintance turned to her and said, "With Grant away for so long, do you not feel like having an affair?" Her typical reply was, "I don't have any ******* time"! Father returned in 1945 and I think it must have been a difficult adjustment for the whole family. My younger brother ,Bill, aged three had become Master of the house!

My father always said she was a wonderful wife and mother. He was desperately in need of a home after his parents died and this is just what Mother gave him – a welcoming, comfortable refuge with good food and a good routine. My mother could be described in the German as Kinder, Küche and Kirke – children, kitchen and church. She loved her home and her children and was a very faithful and hardworking member of the Christian church.

Alison and family

She devoted her life to all three plus her husband! She did a huge amount for him, having lunch ready for him every day when he rushed back between clinics, entertaining overseas postgrad students – always an open house. When I was eleven, we moved to a larger house on the outskirts of Edinburgh. I never liked this house as much as the last one. Dad chose this one and it turned out to be a burden for Mother. I always felt she was stressed out keeping the house clean and tidy (which he would have expected). Mother stoked the coke central heating boiler, cleared the drive of snow, and mowed the grass until he did it. Then he bought a motor mower! She did have a series of domestic helps – Mrs Sinclair, a large quiet woman, and Pinkie (Mrs Pinkerton), who was a real character and certainly contributed to my education! She had a deep dislike of Catholics ("Thae Catholics!", she would mutter). We sometimes had 'live-in maids' – Joey, who was found by us in the kitchen purportedly making money with her boyfriend who was a soldier at the local barracks, and Phemie (Euphemia) her cousin who, after my father had had a word with her boyfriend, married him!

84

Not only did Mother have all of us to care for, she also, being the only sibling nearby, did a great deal for her mother and father. Her mother lived a 5-minute drive up the road and her father was in hospital outside Edinburgh. Mother did have outside interests – she was a good golfer and created a stir on the Baberton golf course by hitting a ball

Grant and Alison Peterkin.1973

up a sheep's bottom. She commented about some of her golfing colleagues – "she had a 'card and pencil' look" meaning they were obsessed with their score cards. She was also chairman of the local Conservative party where she helped to get Lord John Hope into Parliament. She was a good public speaker. She also played the piano in old folks' homes. Having had a rather depressing day in one of them, she declared that she never wanted to be old. She never was! She died aged 67. She was a warm compassionate and loving lady. She brought us up with a good sense of right and wrong and she would never say anything behind peoples' backs that she would not be prepared to say to their faces. She was more at home with the common man than with the "high heid yins". She would have preferred in some ways to have been the wife of a country GP than that of a medical specialist. She managed to live long enough to see all her children happily married. When I finally met my match and she saw me off at the altar, she remarked, "Now, let thy servant depart in peace". She could die happily knowing her children were not going to be alone in life's journey. She had the pleasure of meeting three of what would be eight grandchildren.

In 1962, she found a ground and basement flat in the centre of Edinburgh. It had a small garden reached by going through the bathroom on the basement floor. The kitchen, dining room and two bedrooms were located on that floor and, on the ground floor, there was a large drawing room looking onto beautiful private gardens, my parents' bedroom, a study and a bathroom. It was a great deal easier to keep than the last house although the layout was awkward by modern standards as it meant Mother was deep down in the kitchen while my father relaxed in the drawing room. Occasionally, my father would see patients at home and they were ushered into the study. My brother, whilst studying medicine, lived in one of the bedrooms in the basement which had an entrance beside it. Here he would smuggle in girlfriends hoping my mother would not hear. There was one occasion when she appeared to say good night. Vicky, his future wife, had to be hidden in the wardrobe!

Mother's last years were taken up with treatment for cancer.(caused by her smoking) The radiotherapy had left her gullet very narrow and she suffered being unable to swallow properly. I was living in England at that point and came to help her after a bout of radiotherapy. I was pregnant with Robert. She was always concerned that I would overdo it and chased me back down south after a couple of weeks. "Your place is with your husband," she told me firmly. She was always concerned for others. Dad treated me to a First Class carriage and I was so glad of it as I cried all the way to London not knowing if I would see her again. She rallied a bit and managed to come south for our new baby Robert's christening. Nine months later, she went into hospital to have an operation on her gullet to widen it. It was a hospital she had been in before and hated it. She said the care was appalling and the atmosphere bleak. And here she was again having had a stroke. Dad rang us and said we needed to come quickly as she was very ill. I left Robert with Bill and rushed north. Anne arrived with her 3-month-old baby Frances and left her other child with her husband. We didn't recognise our mother – totally changed – her face was contorted and her hair unkempt trailing over the pillow. Tears poured down our cheeks. Dad was in deep distress. Mum had another stroke and fell into a coma. She never came out of it. I wanted to stay with her but Dad seemed to think there was no point. We were reliant on him for transport though, looking back, we could have got taxis. He wanted to get home and could not really face seeing his wife like that. It was a hard time. We were young and inexperienced. Looking back now, I would have done things differently. It was hard for my sister coping with a new baby with all this going on. Father could not face the prospect of losing his wife; both his parents had died when he was seventeen and his brother and sister had both died relatively young. So, it was not surprising that he could not cope with the death of another loved one. (He used to quote "timor mortis conturbat me"- he had a great fear of death) It was a hard time for all of us. I was in deep shock and did not grieve properly for my mother till years later when it all spilled out at the Family Reunion when we prayed for those "who were not with us". I wept copiously!

It was a packed funeral service for Mother in The Dean Church and later at Warriston Crematorium which I hated and to which

I have never been back. As we got into the funeral car, old cousin Nancy tapped on the window. Bill remarked that the old dear was hitching a lift to the Crem. We burst out laughing which may not have seemed appropriate to lookers-on! Our mother was a brave unselfish lady who lived for her family and would be very proud and delighted to see how the family has kept together and looked out for one another. She died at the age of 68 – much younger than her ancestors and siblings.

CHAPTER 11

Dora's Story as Told to Her Daughter, Alison

"Things my mother told me!" Mother being Dora Gilbert Tucker (nee Elder)

Born on 15th October 1909 in the Manse of the Forman United Free Church, Leven, Fife, Dora was the fifth of six children. Growing up she was kept in her place by three older sisters! Despite a gap of four years between her and the youngest, Patricia, she was held back for "nursery tea", etc., to keep Pat company. She remembers spending wet Sunday afternoons tucked into a little alcove halfway up the stairs reading aloud to herself. Hannah and Hugo both had small bedrooms to themselves. The other four were together in a large L-shaped room which they referred to as "the slum", much to their mother's annoyance. As the eldest, Jenny had the room in the 'L' bit. Pat, who in the early years went to bed earlier, had to cope with the bright light in the middle of the room. Evidently, this caused a long-term habit of her sleeping with her arm across her eyes. Jenny and Dora were great gigglers and were often told off by Alison who was trying to get to sleep herself!

Hannah and Jenny both learned the violin and Alison the piano. When it came to Dora, she was started on the cello as this was needed for quartet-playing! In one way, this was not practical as she had small hands, but cello playing gave her years of pleasure. (She was still playing quartets with friends until she was ninety and had moved to Coldstream.)

For a number of years, the family used to take a cottage on Arran for two months in the school summer holidays (their father was there for one month). They had to take a large amount of paraphernalia including golf-clubs and bikes.

Dora Elder 1928 St Georges School

Languages were not Dora's forte. To pass the General Certificate (or whatever it was then), you had to pass in all subjects. The first time round, Dora failed French. The second time around, she passed everything – except French again! Latin was no better. Hugo was asked to coach her, and his method was to have a pin on the end of a pencil ready to stick into her thigh whenever she made a mistake. With Dora having one eye on the pin and the other on the book, the result was that Hugo told Mother she would never be any good at it. The plan was abandoned!

Dora had two particular friends at St George's. In their final year, Margaret was head girl, Dora was vice-head and Winnie was Senior Prefect; a strong triumvirate.

On leaving school, Dora gave more time to her music – piano, cello and singing. She also did a domestic training course at Atholl Crescent. This was so she could help her mother at home and save on domestic staff but, in the long term, it turned out to be the best training for her future role as Headmaster's wife at Rockport School…

In July 1936, Dora married Eric Tucker. Eric and Hugo had rooms on the same staircase in Corpus Christi in Oxford. Eric started his four-year Classics Degree course at the same time as Hugo started in third

Rockport 1947

year, having already taken his degree in Edinburgh. Hugo invited Eric for New Year 1930/31 to stay at the Manse in Moffat. From then on, Eric came regularly twice a year for a holiday to the Moffat Manse. He enjoyed the golf and the company! After he finished at Oxford and started teaching at Rockport, he used to arrange to go to Ireland via Moffat, crossing on the ferry from Glasgow to Belfast. (This went on for several years as a young Prep School master was in no position financially to marry for some time). However, The Day finally arrived! Dora and Eric went on to have three daughters- Alison, Rosalind and Sheila. They also had innumerable 'sons'– pupils of Rockport School whom Dora mothered and cared for in her role as Headmaster's wife. She worked tirelessly in that role and the school was her home. When Eric retired, they moved to their house up the road, Greenloaning. Later, when Eric died, at the age of eighty-nine she moved to Coldstream to be near her daughter Alison. She lived to the ripe old age of 103.

Rockport School had a huge influence on the extended family. This beautiful Georgian house set in large grounds overlooking Belfast Loch became a home for some of the cousins and a holiday place for the rest of us. For several summers, the cousins from South Africa, Canada, Scotland and England crossed the Irish Sea to Belfast. It was an exciting journey and we all looked out to see if we could see Rockport from the boat. Sometimes the Captain would blow the hooter to announce our arrival. Rockport, being a boarding school, had dormitories to which we were allocated. The girls were on one floor and the boys on another, each large room split into wooden cabins with two beds in each. At the end of the dormitory was a room for the teacher in charge. In this case, it would be one of the aunts. Alison 'volunteered 'to supervise our dorm and she was quickly nick -named MA MURPHY. The facilities were amazing – tennis courts, ponies, the Loch to swim in and plenty of space for organizing dramas, music, plays, etc. We ran wild! Along the road was a golf course for the adults. Dora was ever-welcoming. Fortunately, she had the school cooks and domestic staff whom she had to employ during the school holidays. This was her home, and we ran riot in it. It was these holidays at Rockport that created life-long bonds between the cousins and indeed led to the **Elder Reunions in 1989 and 2002** mentioned below.

Another great event which led to the cousins meeting up again was the **100th birthday of Dora**. There was a great turnout of the Robertsons, Gillian and Bill and spouses from Canada, Hugh Elder and spouse from London, two Parks, Catherine and Malcolm from

South Africa, three Peterkins – Anne and spouse, Allie and spouse and Bill and spouse – three Hursts, Martyn, Hugh and Patrick and spouses, and three Tuckers, Alison, Rosalind, Sheila and spouses. The whole event was organized by Alison and her family, and it was a wonderful weekend of chat and laughter, food and drink.

DORA'S 100TH BIRTHDAY
Aunt Do has time with the cousins

Bill Robertson

Patrick Hurst

Bill and Vicky Peterkin

Anne and David Bolam

Elder Hugh

Catherine and Malcom Park

Gordon Tams

Gordon and Alison working hard to make the weekend
such a great success

While at Victoria Lodge, then aged 101, Dora was present at an afternoon of reminiscing about school days. *The contributions were made into a booklet. This is hers… "I am an Edinburgh lass! I went to St George's Girls School in Edinburgh. It was a l-o-n-g time ago!! I was very happy at school and we did a lot of singing – I sang in the school choir. I also played the cello in the school orchestra; I attended a chamber music class every week. In later life, I played in the Belfast Philharmonic Orchestra. I was Vice-Head Girl at school. I was the fifth out of six children, so I was a very small and insignificant person! I had bossy elder sisters. One sister played the piano, another played the violin, so we played as a trio."*

At this point, I finally found my mother's version (when I was looking for something else – as so often happens). So, I will now type my mother's version before the ink fades completely …
(Pieces in italics are my additions)

Our home was 33 Inverleith Terrace, Edinburgh. A large family house, semi-detached, with a garden, front, side and back. We moved there in 1910 when our father was appointed minister of Stockbridge Church. By then, there were five in the family and Grandfather Macainsh thought the Stockbridge Manse would not be big enough for us. Also, I believe it wasn't in too pleasant an area, so Grandfather bought 33 Inverleith Terrace. Downstairs were three living rooms, one a study, a large kitchen and back kitchen. In this was a large clothes boiler which was lit on Monday to do the family wash! This was done by Mrs Hogg who came on Mondays and Tuesdays. The sheets, etc., were put through a mangle! The ironing was done with "flat irons". Those were heated on a special stove for the purpose. Care had to be taken for heat and smuts from the fire in the stove. (*The laundry included the homemade, reusable sanitary towels. Think of it; five girls! The special laundry bag must always have been in use. Poor Mrs Hogg!*) Off the kitchen, a stair went up to a bedroom for the domestic helpers. We had two; a cook and a housemaid.

On the first floor of the house, there was a large L-shaped drawing room. The piano was in the L-part. This was primarily Mother's room, and I have a vivid picture of her sitting beside a cosy coal fire. She always seemed to be there when you came home from school, ready to listen to your joys and problems.

There were three double bedrooms on that floor, a large linen cupboard and one bathroom – the only one for the house! There was a loo in the cloakroom downstairs. One of these bedrooms had to be a guest room, for friends, but mostly for the visiting ministers who were taking the services at the weekend. No one had a car in those days, so guests had to stay the night. This meant that the parents had their bedroom and Jenny, Alison, Dora and Pat had to share the remaining room. This was large with an L-shape off the main room. Jenny had that with a curtain and a bedlight! The other three of us had to fit into the rest of the room and, as you can imagine, it was not very tidy. We called it "The Slum", much to Mother's annoyance!

Hannah was the privileged eldest! She had a lovely room up a stair. As she was at University, she had to have peace to study! The rest of us did our homework in the Parlour downstairs. What about Hugo? He had a very small room upstairs beside Hannah which he treasured as his own domain!

As we were all out during the day, the evening meal was our meeting place, and we sat down, eight of us, round the dining-room table. We each had our own place (*Dora was beside her father. She told me exactly who sat where, but I can't remember the others!)* Many were the discussions and arguments around that table. As long as it was possible, and it had to stop eventually when we had evening commitments, we had family prayers after our meal – a Bible reading and a prayer.

We had wonderful parents. They were strict and DUTY was a very important thing. You had to do what was required before what you wished. But with all that, there was so much love and concern, and interest in all that we did. Their training and example have stood by me all my long life. I don't remember much social life. Mother and Dad were busy with church commitments. They weren't socially inclined; more taken up with the family, but most welcoming to our friends and anyone they thought might be lonely.

When Dad moved to Moffat in 1930, the Manse there was open house to their friends and our friends during the holidays from University and College. Archie Elder, our first cousin, was a very welcome and frequent visitor to the Manse *(in Moffat)*. He and Eric Tucker were a very light-hearted pair and there was much fun and laughter. Many golf matches were played with Hugo and his friend, Dick Evers. Hugo and Dick were "The Prees" and Archie and Eric were "The Chums", Chortlebury and Chumbleby.

We lived within easy walking distance of Edinburgh Academy, a well-known boys' school, and Hugo spent all his schooldays there. Having passed the required Entrance Exams, he went on to Edinburgh University where he attained a first class Honours Degree in Classics. From there, he went to Corpus Christi College, Oxford for two years and attained a second class Honours degree in Classics.

Aunt Dora

For some time past, there had been a strong movement to provide better schools for girls known as "Schools for the Further Education of Women." St George's School for Girls in Murrayfield was one of them and all five of us went there. The only practical way of getting there was by walking or cycling the one- and three-quarter miles. This we did all our school days; for most of us, this was thirteen years! (*As a five-year-old, Dora started by riding on the back of Hannah's bike.*) The front door of number 33 had a large porch, and the bicycles were stacked on either side. (*There was one bike rack and the newest bike used that; the rest were piled anyhow.*) Rather untidy, and we wondered in hindsight why Dad had never got a hut or shed in the back garden to house the bicycles!

If the weather was a bit wet, we walked to school. If it was very wet, we went in a horse-drawn cab! I used to feel sorry for the driver who had to sit out in the rain!

St George's was a fine school with many facilities. Hockey was played in the Christmas term, lacrosse in the Spring term and cricket and tennis in the summer.

Mother had a theory that hockey was bad for a girl's deportment as one had to bend over all the time while hitting the ball. This meant we couldn't play so didn't have any games in the Christmas term. By the time Pat had reached that age, her older sisters took a deputation to Mother on Pat's behalf to allow her to play hockey!

This was successful with the result that Pat not only played hockey but reached the 1st Eleven team!

The time span from when Hannah started at St George's until Pat finished was 21 years. When Pat left, our parents presented the school with a silver cup – The Elder Cup. This was for singing, choral or solo, to be competed for annually.

Allie Writes: I used to visit Aunt Do when she moved to Coldstream and it was always such a pleasure to reminisce with her about the family and as with all my aunts there was always such a warm welcome. I was always amazed at how she adapted at eighty nine to a completely new life in the Borders.

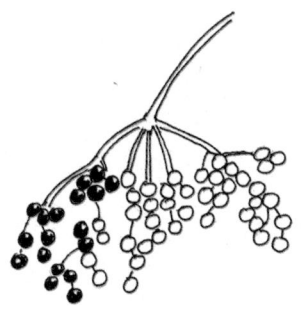

CHAPTER 12

The Youngest and Sixth Child, Patricia

Her Story was written in her eulogy by Andrew Hurst, her husband

Patricia's story is divided into four phases.

The first phase consists of the first 25 years of her life. Patricia was born on the 12ᵗʰ of January 1914, a few months before the outbreak of the Great War. Her father was the Reverend Hugh Elder, a minister of the Church of Scotland; her mother was a daughter of the Manse. She was the seventh child of the seventh child and therefore, by Scottish tradition, a little fey. She was brought up in a loving, comfortable and happy, but not indulgent home in that agreeable part of Edinburgh, Inverleith Terrace, which lies between the Botanical Gardens and the Water of Leith. She followed her four elder sisters to St George's, the well-known Edinburgh Girls' School, and went from there to Edinburgh University, where she took her MA degree and also found time to become President of the Women's Union (The Talking Women as they were called) and to represent the University at tennis, golf, hockey and lacrosse.

From there, she took off for London, where she acquired a Secretarial training and was introduced by a friend to the film

London

industry, where she was just becoming noticed for some of her reports, when she left to accompany her parents to South Africa and Rhodesia for a sister's wedding. On returning, she found her brother had been appointed as the new young headmaster of Dean Close School, Cheltenham, and she was persuaded to join him there as Chatelaine of the School House and Headmaster's secretary. There she was, just as a young and lively newcomer, finding her way into Cheltenham society when the Second World War broke out, and Dean Close's buildings were requisitioned at short notice by the Admiralty and the whole school moved, lock, stock and barrel, to Somerset where the Governors of Monkton Combe School near Bath took them in, and where, at the time, I was a young schoolmaster about the same age as Patricia, and just down from Oxford.

This is the end of phase one of Patricia's life. She had grown up from a little girl – perhaps you can imagine her with a cut-down golf club in her hands, riding her beloved pony in the wild places of the Isle of Arran where her family migrated each year for two months of the long Scottish summer holiday, and then

Patricia

in 1939, as a very lively and attractive young woman of 25 years of age. This first phase was **HER** life. For the next 65 years, it was not only her life, but also **their** life.

The second stage of her life started in 1940 and lasted for a decade. It was full of excitement, change, movement, adventure, high romance, comedy, tragedy and even a dash of farce. It started with Patricia in the unusual – indeed, I should think, unique – position of being secretary to the headmaster of two public boarding schools at the same time. It ended 10 years later with her as the still very attractive young mother of 3 sons. The first year was for her – us – the most exciting and eventful of our lives. Here are a couple of incidents from its early days:

Now you will all have seen Dad's Army on television. Well, Andrew was actually a founder member of Dad's Army by virtue of being a Territorial Army Officer not yet on active service, and he assures us that the BBC Version is completely authentic. Indeed, his CO at Monckton Combe was not unlike Captain Mannering. Once a week, at the end of the school day, which, in a public boarding school is about 10 pm, he would take six cadets from the School OTC and lead them up to the top of the local hillside where they had already dug trenches. There they would sit for the rest of the night with fixed bayonets waiting to defend Somerset against the expected German invasion – but – before that, Andrew would have led his party down into the village to Patricia's lodgings, rapped sharply with my own bayonet on a convenient drainpipe to tell her they had arrived and then escorted her to a neighbouring hillside to join a party of ladies who were watching for parachutists (Germans possibly disguised as nuns we were told). Patricia confided to me later that she had some difficulty in avoiding the bayonets of her escort. At the end of term Concert in the Christmas Term, her last contribution to Monkton Combe was a highly popular skit embroidering, in her own particular way that they all remember, the true-life incident when the rifle of the biology master was discharged within inches of the CO's ear.

Patricia

And then, in the early June of their by now somewhat hilarious summer term, a little before Dunkirk, a visitor arrived in Bath for Patricia in the person of a tea-planter on leave from the Dutch East Indies, hoping to take her back with him to Sumatra as his wife. Andrew assumed he must be her fiancé from Scotland or some such thing, but anyway, one day, they were sitting at the High Table in the School Dining Hall, and enjoying the excellent dinner that Monkton Combe still provided in spite of rationing, when the School butler, a man of some discretion, came up to the table and whispered in Patricia's ear, "Miss Elder, it's the other gentleman on the telephone". This has always been one of Patricia's favourite little stories, of which, as we all know, she had many.

The other gentleman, doubtless much to his great regret, departed back to Sumatra alone, but the story has a happy ending. After two years in a Japanese prisoner of war camp, and surviving many hardships, he eventually returned safely to Andrew's parent's home, and there, in the 1960s, Martyn, Hugh and even his father helped him in with the harvest and Patricia and he used to exchange visits with him and his wife.

Neither Patricia nor Andrew, in those early summer days of 1940, had the slightest idea that they would be engaged within a month, and married a month later, though the school was not wholly surprised as there is very little privacy in a public boarding school, and most of what one does is visible to two or three hundred pairs of alert and interested eyes. At Easter 1940, the Admiralty found that they no longer needed Dean Close buildings so the school had returned to Cheltenham for the summer term, leaving Patricia at Monkton, as her brother Hugo was now married. So, the big day of her life arrived and they were married twice on August 10th 1940, once in the morning at the Registrar's Office and again (our real wedding) in the afternoon in Dean Close School Chapel (at that time not licensed for weddings). Patricia liked to remember the look on the Registrar's face when she returned the ring to Andrew at the end of the first ceremony. Her father could not leave Edinburgh so the Reverend Hayward, Headmaster of Monkton Combe took the Service in Dean Close School Chapel, assisted by Hugo, and his wife Mary was Matron of Honour. It was the height of the Battle of Britain, Andrew's parents had difficulty in leaving Suffolk, and it was the actual day originally intended by Hitler for the invasion (Operation Sealion Day).

Then a night at their favourite hotel, The Cross Hands, midway between Bath and Cheltenham, at Old Sodbury and off to South Devon where, on their first night there, enemy planes sank the dredger in Brixham Harbour, and set fire to the oil storage tanks on Berry Head, about three miles from our attractive country hotel,

105

which they had more or less to themselves because of the bombing, and in spite of petrol rationing, they had plenty for their little Austin Seven, thanks to the good will of their friends, and even the hotel which gave them precious coupons.

Patricia wedding photo

All good things come to an end, and after a fortnight in Devon, and then Somerset, Oxford and Suffolk, Patricia returned to Edinburgh and Andrew reported to Aldershot from where he watched the glare of London burning as the blitz started the very next day – the end of their midsummer madness, as Patricia liked to call it. During the month or two in the south, when he was guarding Chequers and Bomber Command with a platoon from a young soldier's battalion of the Royal Berkshire Regiment, she spent a clandestine night with him in his quarters and it was then off to the Royal Artillery at Newcastle upon Tyne, where, for a year or so, she described herself as 'a camp follower with benefit of clergy'. She could hardly subsist on the three shillings a day which was a subaltern's marriage allowance at the time, so she answered an advertisement for an experienced governess and spent the next few months riding about the estate of her employer with her two charges, back for safety reasons from Wycombe Abbey; playing tennis with the Brigadier and my Colonel on the tennis courts at our HQ, which had formerly been a women's teachers' training college; or keeping open house for her new husband and his officer colleagues in her bed-sitting room.

She also enrolled as an Air Raid Warden (Newcastle was quite a target for the bombers, as they were building the battleship King George V and the aircraft carrier Anson on the Tyne). Despite the bombs, the only casualty to either of them was the day that she was reaching up for her steel helmet (tin hat as we called them) and, shaken by the vibration of one of our heavy guns going off nearby, it was dislodged from where it was on top of the wardrobe and fell on her head, fortunately without damage (friendly fire we would call it nowadays).

And so ended their first year together, because at the end of the Summer of 1941, the Headmaster of Merchiston Castle School, Edinburgh, a few hundred yards from her mother's house at Colinton, needed a part-time secretary. In our circumstances, it was an opportunity not to be missed. So Patricia left Newcastle and their happy interlude there was over. Martyn was born in September 1942 and Andrew applied to leave my job as a Gun

Patricia

Control Officer and returned to regimental duty with Light Anti-Aircraft guns and, before long, was in India. So it was goodbye once again, this time for three years. Her father was said to have remarked, "What a disaster" when he heard of Martyn's birth so you can imagine Patricia's pleasure and that little smile again when she next saw him and said, "Meet the disaster".

Of course, at that time, they would have given much for a few years together, perhaps even settled for less than ten. So many of their friends, and some of the boys Andrew taught, never came back, but we were lucky and the three years passed. He progressed from 2nd Lieutenant to Major. Patricia flew over in a biplane to help her sister Dora in Northern Ireland. The Japanese surrendered, and they were reunited in the Spring of 1946 and spent the summer of that year on leave in the tumbledown cottage. Shore Cottage, as it was called, was kindly lent to them by Dora and Eric Tucker, now back from the Royal Corps of Signals and Headmaster/owner of Rockport, the number-one prep school in Northern Ireland. There were absolutely no facilities, and water was brought down by me in buckets from the school. Cooking was in an old range with wood collected from the estate. The conveniences were about fifty yards down the wild garden. Light was provided by oil lamps. Heating was not required in the summer. Andrew can remember a real crisis when a party of hikers along the shore asked for a drink of water and reduced them to about nothing. It was hardly more comfortable than his tent in the jungle in India, but of course, it was also a little bit of paradise.

And then off to Exeter. It was difficult in those days, just after the war, to find a satisfactory place to live, so a few rooms near the Cathedral saw us through the autumn Term at Exeter School, and then after a family Christmas reunion at Sudbury, Patricia returned to Edinburgh, where Hugh was born in February 1947, and on her return at Easter, they moved into our first home together in the

Old Rectory in the village of Sowton, where they had the whole of the top floor of what had been a Georgian mansion, and two vast living rooms on the ground floor, and where Patrick was born eighteen months later, just after Andrew had been appointed Divisional Education Officer at Amersham. So, another six months of separation, with Patricia still at the Rectory and him in Buckinghamshire. And that is the end of the second phase of Patricia's life. It was full of excitement and change; they started off beside Bath and went on to Newcastle, Edinburgh, India, Ireland and Exeter and now Amersham.

Phase 3 is the story of a house – Trees, Stanley Hill, Amersham. They were very lucky indeed to find it in those days when there was an absolute dearth of any houses at all, let alone one with plenty of accommodation, and it was through the generosity of Patricia's mother that they were able to afford the mortgage. Trees was quite a big house with plenty of space and standing in an acre of garden, half of which was wild: a jungle to their sons, and a park to some of her pupils. But it was much more than just a house – it was, by turns and often at the same time, a HOME, a hostel, a hotel, a school, a theatre and even occasionally a nursing home, and there, for the next 33 years, Patricia presided over a succession of activities and influenced many lives.

Her first action on moving in was to set aside a room for what she called her PG, a young woman who was pleased to find somewhere pleasant to live, and at a small rent in exchange for babysitting. This was essential at the time, as Andrew had been made acting Warden of Missenden Abbey which required him to leave my office at midday on Friday and stay at the Abbey until after lunch on

Sunday and Patricia was expected to act as hostess from time to time, possibly for a course of 100 or so teachers. One of the girls who stayed with us at Trees is still sending Christmas cards this year, 50 years later. Patricia devoted the next few years to bringing up our family, at the same time keeping open house for numerous friends and relations and entertaining a range of sometimes quite distinguished visitors. Each year, when Lady Meyer came down to preside over the School's Music Festival at Chesham, she took her back to Trees after the formal lunch to rest until the evening concerts, and sent her back to London with great armfuls of lilac from the garden. One day, it was the wife of the Lord Chancellor down to open one of my new schools. Another time, Arthur Bryant, the historian, said one of our dogs suspected him of going off with the spoons, and Patricia received one of his books, "The Dog in My Life", a few days later.

It was always a matter of great regret that all her four sisters lived far away – Canada, Rhodesia, Northern Ireland and Scotland – so the house was often full during their sometimes quite long visits, and hardly ever without one or more of our numerous nieces and nephews staying. Then there was a succession of children's friends first from school, then from Oxford and St Andrew's Universities, and of course the Officer Cadets from Henlow and Cranwell whom Martyn brought down to Trees. Indeed, our courtyard was hardly ever free from the oil slicks which resulted from their seemingly never-ending attention to their ancient sports cars.

Patricia loved entertaining. Then again, it seems amazing looking back to think that every school day morning for 25 years, the house was full of children. This was the Amersham Home Group, which she invented and sustained until she retired in 1979. Trees was also a base for adventures elsewhere. From there, our little family set off, year after year, to spend a month or so of the summer holiday with Patricia's sister Dora and her husband Eric at Rockport Preparatory School in Northern Ireland. There was tennis, golf, swimming, fishing, the Giant's Causeway, the Mountains of Mourne, a resident pony and a cordial welcome from the school and the adjacent royal Belfast Golf Club. Trees was a base too for us when we were watching Martyn play in various places as Hooker for the RAF Rugby side, for Hugh on his various travels and for Patrick in the Caribbean or the Congo. Also, for them in later years on our annual cruises with P&O on the School Cruise ships, Nevassa and Uganda, in the Mediterranean. For ten years, they used to take two or three hundred children away for a couple of weeks. Patricia was very popular with the Ship's Officers and great friends with the Dance Band Leader, and Andrew remembers the day in a Force 9 gale when she said there was nobody under fifty above the decks.

Trees was also a base for the visits of Martyn and Sue when they were stationed in Germany and her elder sister Hannah in Canada.

But her special achievement was the establishment and sustaining of the Amersham Home Group, as she called it, to which she gave 25 years of her life – and it all came about by chance. One day in the office, Andrew could not find a teacher anywhere to give home tuition to a boy who was said to be difficult. Our boys were now at school. She was qualified by virtue of her degree to teach but she had never considered teaching as a career. However, she was prepared to have a go. One pupil became three. Why not bring them back to Trees to the deserted playroom? Then they could have three hours each together instead of one separately. Committees approved, the doctors liked the idea, the heads of Schools gave it their support, and soon three had become eight, which was the maximum that the classroom, as it was now, could accommodate. So, for the next quarter of a century, the school transport deposited eight children at our door at 9 am and came to take them back to their normal schools for the afternoon. They were children who had to cope with some physical disability. Patricia taught them (ably assisted by Joan McNab, who was recruited from next door) but she not only taught them, she also helped them to help themselves. There were those who found it difficult to walk, and those who found it difficult to talk. There was the boy who was nearly blind, whom she got into Grammar school. There was a boy recovering from polio, who was ostracised locally by those afraid of catching it. There were those with hearing difficulties, those catching up after illness, and some who had just fallen behind.

Each Christmas, she produced a remarkably watchable panto-mime which gave her and the children great pleasure and there was always considerable competition, especially from the Golf Club La-dies, for one of the limited number of seats for spectators which our drawing and dining rooms allowed. Visits were made to Whipsnade and other places, and I think it was at Woburn where a baboon was only just excluded from the party's transport.

Looking back, I don't think Andrew or the rest of the family realised quite how much of herself she gave in those 25 years of service, but it was really quite something. And, of course, it was concurrent with running a home, large-scale entertaining, and the physical and social environment of Harewood Downs Golf Club where she enjoyed 35 years of regular play and especially enjoyed her time as Captain. She put a lot into her (our) life at Trees and did it with that little smile. Well, Patricia loved Trees, and we had 33 very good years there. For her, they were years of service to family, to friends, to children and with plenty of enjoyment too – holidays, golf, the church, the garden, entertaining – just being at home.

So it was really no surprise that on our last Guy Fawkes evening there, the family found her crying bitterly and the tears falling onto the sausages frying for hotdogs for the grandchildren. And it took Andrew back to one of the rare occasions when he had seen her in tears – nearly forty years before in Dublin where it seemed they might not get into the Horse show to see Colonel Llewellyn jumping Foxhunter(but they did manage it).

So here ends phase three – our rewarding 33 years at Trees – with much left untold.

Phase Four is the tale of a long and enjoyable retirement. Andrew and Patricia both left gainful employment in the autumn of 1979 and, after a couple more years at Trees, moved in January 1982 to Deep Dene. They were both now coming up towards 70, and the days were long gone when Patricia had told Andrew that the two things she would really have liked to have done in her life were to have ridden in the Grand National and to have gone down the Cresta Run. It was now the evening of their lives but days at Deep Dene had been very enjoyable and there was still plenty of life and excitement left. As GK Chesterton puts it so well:

"For there is good news yet to hear and fine things to be seen, before we go to Paradise by way of Kensal Green."

When they moved, they thought they might have 5 years or so to enjoy Deep Dene, which they thought of as their luxury bungalow, but in the event, they extended to ten and then twenty. Their Golden Wedding came and went, their Diamond Wedding arrived, and Patricia much appreciated the formal telegram from the Queen on that occasion. There was travel. The Mediterranean gave way to places further afield. She had flown out to Germany to help when Belinda was born, and then they first met Elizabeth (Hugh and Penny's first-born) in the Botanical Gardens in Christchurch, New Zealand. There were journeys around the world, when they had two very rewarding visits to Hugh and Penny in Australia, going out via America and the South Sea Islands, and returning via Hong Kong, Singapore and Bangkok. There was another visit to Hannah and family in Ontario, and onto the Rockies and the Prairies; a never-to-be-forgotten visit to Egypt with the family; a special train through the Alps, ending up in Corsica and Monte Carlo and the Tower of Pisa. And nearer home, there were numerous holidays with Patrick and family and others to Scotland, especially Dumfries and Galloway. And of course, our many visits to France with Patrick in the south, Martyn in Paris and the Loire and Audrey and Bob in Normandy – not forgetting her annual week with Dora in County Down.

Golf at Harewood continued to be a great pleasure to her, and she discovered, quite late in life, the fascination of the Bridge Table, and Deep Dene was thereafter the setting for many afternoons of Ladies' Bridge. There was now plenty of time for entertainment of friends, relatives, and family and always, Elizabeth had reminded them so nicely, there was an increasing generation of grandchildren, who enjoyed the new house and garden, as their parents and cousins had enjoyed Trees. And then the garden. Deep Dene had four little, more or less separate gardens; the Rose Garden, The Orchard, the formal area of lawn terraces and goldfish pond and the Patio. Patricia looked after the roses and other flowers, tended several generations of goldfish, and enjoyed many sessions of play with our grandchildren in the Orchard and round the winding paths elsewhere. She had her little study indoors with its displays of books and ornaments, and she could watch television programmes with the children or retreat there for the Wimbledon fortnight.

And of course, the dogs were very much a part of her family. Cactus and Thistle came with us from Trees, and Holly, who now much misses the little games that Patricia played with her in the fields, and coaxes me into bringing back some of them, and of course, Judy, Bramble and Thorn in the earlier days.

A visit to Logies from Aunt Pat and Uncle Andrew

And last, but by no means least, the little church at Latimer. The family had grown up with the church at Great Missenden dating from our days at the Missenden Abbey and, when our old friend the Rector retired, we followed Martyn and Sue to Latimer just before they left Trees. Patricia was soon a member of the PCC and expended much time and effort into all sorts of things there: helping with the Annual Fete, cleaning the brasses, arranging flowers and helping to run the parish during a long interregnum between Ministers.

The years went by. The turn of the century came, and that was basically the end of Phase 4. What more is there to say? She fell and broke her leg on the not-so-glorious first of June in the year 2000. She made a good recovery for 2 years, though she never walked again without sticks. They managed two more visits to France; the latter with the help of a nurse, and a rewarding flight to Scotland for the Second Elder Reunion, which Alison Logie organised so successfully at Crieff, and last visit to Kent and a final Christmas in London with Patrick. Then old age took over. She fell again and broke her other leg in July 2003, and she spent the next year in hospital or the Westminster Nursing Home, completely helpless but still retaining the quiet grace that had been one of her great gifts in life.

After a short coma, she died on 29th July 2004, after a long, interesting and fulfilled life to which she had brought so much."

Allie writes:

I probably knew Aunt Pat the best of all the Aunts as I worked in Buckinghamshire for 3 years and lived near her. She was a wonderful support to a young girl starting her first job and there were a few times when I cried on her shoulder. She was a wonderful, warm, fun person always so interested in what the young were doing and always welcoming. It was she who encouraged me to go abroad to teach saying "you'll never get a man in Little Chalfont". I duly signed up for VSO and met my husband on the flight to East Africa. So I owe dear Aunt Pat a great deal. We had some great holidays with her chez Martyn's and Sue's in Carquieranne – lots of laughter and good chat! She and Uncle Andrew travelled north in their 80s to have the honeymoon they never had at St Fillans. They stayed with us en route. She was not well at this stage having had small TIAs and when they got to St Fillans, she took a turn for the worse. Bill, my husband, carried her downstairs to the car. She was a very plucky lady. We had some very memorable times together.

Aunt Dora and Aunt Pat

The Following is Patricia's Letter Written to Her Mother from Dean Close School. 1938

This letter reveals the great humour and wit Patricia had.

H.M.H.'s,

D.C.S.

Chelt.

11th July, 1938.

My dearest Mother, Dad, Jenny and family,

        I am sinking to the lowest depths of family correspondence and making a carbon copy of this letter to save writing it twice. I know that it is shameful, but perhaps you will forgive me when I tell you that before this morning's post came in, Hugo and I were 17 letters behind!

        Well, on a cold wet, bleak and typically Moffatonian Friday afternoon, Hugo and self jerked the society smile into position and emmerged onto the field of play, where the School and O.D.s were busy playing that entirely futile game - cricket. Hugo, if I remember rightly wore the grey, pin stripe, complete with pale flame rosebud, while I shivered fitfully in my navyblue suit. There were a few parents about, mostly wanting to talk business, and Hugo was to be seen being genial but firm on the subject of their respective sons' abilities.

        Later the rain descended and we retired. We had the President of the O.D.s staying, a clergyman (needless to say), and a bit of a stick. Hugo and he went off to the O.D. dinner in Cheltenham, while I had a pleasant, solitary meal mainly of sausage and mash. I contemplated going over to watch the performance of the play which was being given to the School, but funked going alone, though I was told by the Masters the next day, that they would have been delighted to have my company, so I told them in future that they should invite me to such things. Actually I fell asleep at 9,0 p.m. on the drawing room sofa, and woke at 10.6 and went to bed.

        I was most anxious about my wedding hat, as I was determined to wear it, and the weather on Friday night was appalling. However on Saturday, though cold and grey it was not actually raining, so I was able to satisfy my vanity, but had to wear a coat on top of my natty Viennese model!

        I couldn't get into the Chapel till nearly 10.o on Sat. morning, and even then Had to march through a choir practice in order to retrieve the flower vases. However I got the flowers looking not too bad, and sped back to change. Hugo had gone off to meet Sir Thomas, and the train was 20 minutes late! I was pacing the drawing room in a fever, unable to sit down, and thus putting an unnecessary strain on the varicose veins. The v.v.s are a serious problem both to the Headmaster and myself, as after several hours standing we feel our legs beginning to droop, and after all we cannot have them all injected, else where will the blood go when it meets a series of 'No road this way' notices round the knee.

2.

Sir Thomas finally arrived, and seemed glad of the hot coffee which we thrust at him. He also wolfed digestive biscuits. He wasn't a bit terrifying and seemed a pleasant individual. Mr. Yeaman also came to coffee, and as there was to be a male only procession over to the Marquee, I was turfed out of the house at about 11.45 all, all, alone. I went over to the field and couldn't see an single person I knew. It was frightful, and I decided that I had better go into the Marquee than present a pathetic figure to the company in general. Needless to say I went in the wrong end of the Marquee, thus leaving myself the whole length of the place to walk. However I seized on one of the Prefects that I knew, and dared him to desert me until I had reached the correct seat. When I reached it, there was no one within rows, and I sat there, endeavouring to look nonchalant. (I seize every available chance of writing that word, as I never have the courage to pronounce it.) Well I sat there idly reading my programme - which I already knew by heart - and presently espied some of the Masters out on the field. As it was obviously going to be ages before the proceedings started, I determined to get out of the place, so I rose to my feet and strolled out of the Marquee as if I owned it. Once out I more or less broke into a run, and rushing upon a group of Masters said in a desperate voice "For goodness' sake, speak to me". I was told that the only reason I had come out of the marquee was in order to make a second and more impressive entry. However, on that I promptly became the Headmaster's sister and quelled the speaker with a steely eye. Frederick Westcott (the music master) asked me if he might be allowed to remark on my smart appearance. This in the world of fiction might be the rise of the curtain on a great drama as his wife is some years older than him and looks more. (Pass the milk, please). However Tuckwell, later in the day, when asked to describe me by XXXXXXXXXXXXX Lady Norwood, said that I had a hat with holes round the edge! These bachelors! However I told him that his dog was exactly like a hedgehog, so honours are even.

Seeing that by this time Mrs. Yeaman XXXXXXXX had now arrived, I made my second entry and greeted her with great joy. Presently the Procession arrived, Hugo respøendent in morning clothes under his gown.

The only flaw in Hugo's speech was when the microphone started hurling his words back at him. That only lasted for about 10 seconds, and otherwise it was a perfect performance. He really made a great sensation, as people came rushing up to me, and said "How proud of your brother you must be", and I was. Poor old Sir Thomas had a heavy row to hoe coming after him, as he himself more or less said. There was just the right amount of humour, and he (Hugo) delivered it beautifully. I shall not say more, as, much against my will, he will probably start reading this letter, despite his protestations on the subject of the privacy of the individual! Also, though there is little fear of it, owing to my blows with

3.

a sledge hammer, I do not wish him to develop a tête-montée (for translation see Pip, by Ian Hay page 46)

After the prize giving which was got through in record time, I flew over to the School kitchens - a promise to Miss Pruen - and admired everything prepared for the Big Lunch. I complemented the Cook, congratulated the head tablemaid on the floral decorations, and was generally smarmy! I catapulted back into our hall and nearly crashed into a stalwart and stout figure in black. "Do you know who I am" came a deep voice from the gloom. A moment's pause, and then slipping back into the well-rehearsed smile, I murmured - "Ah, Cousin Janet, but how charming of you to come over". She moved slightly to one side, and I then espied a wraith like figure. "And Miss Beal, too. You must stay to lunch", said I thinking of my half pound of cold ham and tongue, and modicum of soup of which Miss Pruen and I had planned to have a picnic meal. However they had planned to go back by an early train, and withnpromises xxxx xxxxxxxi that we would most certainly go over in September and see them, I shoed them gently into a taxi.

I then found a group of Governors, who were all terribly thrilled with Hugo, so I stood and chatted to them. They are a very nice set of old fellows and very easy to get on with. We were joined by Sir Thomas, also Lord Dickinson, for whom, in addition to my three guests I had to provide a room to rest.

To me came a lady whom I had called on and had forgotten her name, and said "It's very naughty of my uncle, but he insists that we stay to lunch". Rather a vague remark, don't you think, except for the fact that they intended to stay for lunch. I gathered shortly that Sir Thomas was the Uncle, so explaining that the School lunch was male only, I explained that her husband would have lunch in School, and that I would be delighted if she would have it with me and Miss Pruen. She was very charming and a most easy guest. I parked her in the drawing room and sped to the kitchen. I instructed Cook to tip some more milk into the tomato soup, and rescue the ham that was intended for Sunday nights veal and ham pie, and to open a tin of pineapple, put it in individual dishes with a blob of cream on top. What with coffee and biscuits and cheese and salad we had quite a pleasant lunch. But, oh dear, what a moment.

All afternoon I tramped round with Hugo desperately making conversationnto whichever parent was not bubbling over about their son. Chiefly I got the father, which proves my suspicion that Mothers are inclined to be interfering. (May I add, that this thought has sprung in no degree or particular from my own family life, but from the stupid, verbose and badly constructed letters addressed to the Headmaster which it is my duty to file)

I managed to find some most delightful parents and had tea with them. There was Pa, Ma, and daughter all very amusing, and I was having a high old time. Hugo xxxxxxxi descended upon me

4.

and said that Sir Cyril and Lady Norwood had arrived. We went to
the other end of the Marquee, and I shook hands with Lady N.
Owing to the fact that I was wearing my hat at a very rakish angle,
I didn't see Sir Cyril, and nearly shook hands with someone quite
different! We sat and chatted and then I took them over to the
house. She is simply charming and most motherly and kind, and
by Sunday I felt perfectly at ease with her. He is a very nice
man too, rather silent and therefore a bit overpowering to begin
with. I settled Lady Norwood comfortably in the drawing room,
and went out to plunge into the fray again. I had promised
the Science Master to see all the demonstrations in the labs. so
went round there. I thought I would never get away, as I was
seized on all sides by earnest young scientists who were most
eager to demonstrate their particular thing. I didn't understand
one word of it, but they seemed quite pleased. One was making
balloons, and the one he did for me had a huge hole in it! However
I remarked that demonstrations always went wrong, didn't they, and
passed on to some frightful gadget which showed the density of oil,
or something.

I then joined Hugo on the field, and as we were dining at
7.0, we retired at 6.30. I dashed up to change when there came
a knock at my door, and Cook came in with a face as long as a horse,
and almost in tears. "Oh, Miss Elder" she said, "I've just looked
at the menu you wrote, and I've made to-morrow's dinner, instead
of to-night's, at least the first course." This meant cold anchovy
eggs instead of hot fish cream, and as we were only having a 3
course dinner because of the play at 8.15, I had now two cold
courses and one hot. "Well, never mind" I said, "but we'll have
to have a savoury now", so we had scrambled egg and tomato. It
really was a frightful moment, and I felt like creeping into bed!
All went off all right, and we set off for the play with endless
coats and wraps. It wasn't as cold as I expected, and my long
evening coat was most useful, as I wore an unseen cardigan underneath.

The play was simply magnificent - a most finished production,
and being outside provided just the right setting. All the caste
were very good, and Tuckwell as Falstaff magnificent.

We intended to have him and Phair into tea (both in the play)
after, but they couldn't come. However as there were our three
guests and the mole, we had quite a big party.

I must say I was thankful to roll into bed though I didn't
sleep too well. Poor Hugo had to get up for early service at 8.0,
but I decided to wait until this week, when the Bishop is coming,
and I would have to go anyway.

The morning service at which Sir Cyril preached was
absolutely beautiful. The Chapel was packed with extra benches,
and there were people in the vestry. Hugo read the second lesson

5.

and read extremely well. Lady Norwood remarked on it. The Head Boy read the first lesson and did it very well too. The mole, I must say, conducts a service beautifully and positively glides about the Chapel, which always amuses me when I think of him leaping all over a tennis court.

The Norwoods left soon after lunch. You can imagine how charming she was when I tell you that I recounted the story of the fish being cooked on the wrong day!

Our other visitor left this morning, and Hugo has been seeing parents since breakfast. I don't know when we shall get all the correspondence done, probably by midnight!

We are having a fairly hectic week, as the Tuckers are coming to tea to-day; we are going to a sherry party to-morrow; having the Bradnacks, Hedley Warr and Tuckwell to dinner on Wednesday; people coming to tea on Thursday; and attending the Ladies College speech day on Friday. Thus the social whirl goes on. Never mind in a burst of energy this morning I planned all the meals until breakfast on Thursday, including the dinner party.

You will see our big splash in the Times, thus proving what wire-pulling and corrupt practices will bring forth. The Correspondent was given a whacking good lunch after word from Sir Thomas. This is of course strictly confidential, and slightly exaggerated, it is, really the fame of the School and the distinguished career and presence of the new Headmaster that produces such columns! The rest of the family will have to fly higher than the mere step up to matrimony, to figure in such a paper as the London, distinct from the Moffat, Times.

Farewell,
Pat.

I have not sent a copy to Dora. Pass this on if you like.
What about matinee patern?

122

CHAPTER 13

What Happened Next? A Synopsis from Dora

HANNAH. She qualified in Medicine at Edinburgh University with degrees in MBChB and DPH. After gaining experience as an assistant GP at Lanark, she then set up her plate as a GP in Comely Bank and had her practice there for several years until her marriage and emigrating to Canada.

(At one home delivery, the baby was not breathing and Hannah, remembering the story of Elijah stretching himself three times across a boy and breathing life into him, did similar with the baby and got it going .... The start of mouth-to-mouth resuscitation, perhaps?)

HUGO. After graduating from Oxford, he was appointed as an Assistant Classics Master at Sherborne School in Dorset. From there, he moved to a post in Fettes School, Edinburgh. From there, he applied for the Headship at Dean Close School, Cheltenham and was appointed. After the war, in 1945, he was appointed Head of Merchant Taylors' School, Northwood. He stayed there till he retired in 1965.

JENNY. After graduating MA at Edinburgh University, she went to the Froebel College (Kindergarten and Primary) Roehampton where she achieved a First-Class Certificate. Her first appointment was at Leeds Girls High School. She was there for several years. Later, she had a post in the Training College at St George's before going to Africa to be married.

ALISON. Not being academic, University was not considered. She was very musical and a beautiful pianist and gained an LRAM in piano teaching. She combined this with teaching Chassevante. This was a method of teaching children to read and write music.

DORA. University did not seem to be the answer and as Mother needed more help at home, she took cooking and baking courses and concentrated on piano, cello and chamber music. After the family moved to Moffat in 1930, much time was spent helping Dad in the parish as well as being the family chauffeur!

PATRICIA. After taking her MA degree at Edinburgh and a secretarial course, she went to London and had one or two different jobs. Later, when Hugo was Headmaster at Dean Close, she was his hostess and housekeeper. During the war, when Dean Close was moved to Monkton Coombe School, she moved with the school as the Dean Close Secretary.

The Marriages

November 1935. Alison married Grant Peterkin.

Alison was beautiful with dark brown hair and very dark eyes. Grant spotted her at a dance and from then on, the romance blossomed. Grant was originally going to be a GP but changed to specialize in Dermatology. This meant his medical studies took longer, with the result they were engaged for three years; a long wait for both of them. They both lived in Edinburgh.

Grant and Alison's wedding

July 1936. Dora married Eric Tucker.

Eric and Hugo had rooms on the same staircase in Corpus Christi in Oxford. Eric started his four-year Classics Degree course at the same time as Hugo started in third year, having already taken his degree in Edinburgh. Hugo invited Eric for New Year 1930/31 to stay at the Manse in Moffat. From then on, Eric came regularly twice a year for a holiday at the Moffat Manse. He enjoyed the golf and the company! After he finished at Oxford and started teaching at Rockport, he used to arrange to go to Ireland via Moffat, crossing on the ferry from Glasgow to Belfast. (This went on for several years as a young Prep School master was in no position to marry for some time. However, The Day finally arrived!)

November 1937. Hannah married Edwin Robertson.

Hannah and Edwin were both studying Medicine at Edinburgh University at the same time. At one time, Edwin was Assistant Surgeon and Hannah Anaesthetist in the same operating theatre. The surgeon was reported to have said he had seen romances blossoming in many places, but never before in an operating theatre! For many years, Edwin was the dark-haired man who first-footed the party at which Hannah was present. New Year after New Year passed and we were surprised there was no engagement announcement. We heard later that Edwin didn't feel he could propose until he was earning a considerable income!

March 1938. Janet (Jenny) married Jack (John) Park.

Jenny was a competent violinist and, when she was living in Leeds, she joined an amateur orchestra. The conductor was Jim (James) Park. He married one of the cellists in the orchestra, and Jenny was often a visitor to their home. Jim had a twin brother Jack who was in the printing business in Bulawayo, S. Rhodesia. Early in 1936, Jack came home to Leeds for a holiday and he and Jenny met at Jim and Barbara's home and spent some time going out together before Jack returned to Rhodesia. In July, Jack proposed to Jenny by letter asking her to go out to Rhodesia to marry him.

After some thought, she accepted him, and brother Jim was commissioned to buy the engagement ring! Jim called himself "the carbon copy"!

Father retired from active ministry early in 1938, and he and Mother and Pat, and Jenny as the "bride-to-be", sailed out to Cape Town. At that time, there were no flights, and the voyage took about three weeks. Jack was waiting for them at Cape Town, and a few days later, Father married them in a church there. While they were on their honeymoon, the other three had a holiday in Rhodesia visiting the Victoria Falls and ending in Bulawayo where Jack and Jenny were going to live.

Their good judgement was rewarded with fifty happy years of marriage.

December 1939. Hugo (Hugh) married Mary Stagg.

One summer in the 1930s, Hugo was invited to a House Party in a large house in Ireland (Eire). There were a number of guests and one of them was a girl from the south of England called Mary Stagg. A friendship ensued between Hugo and Mary which ended in an engagement. They were married in Swanage just at the start of the Second World War. Pat was Mary's bridesmaid and Mary was Pat's matron of honour eight months later.

10th August 1940. Patricia married Andrew Hurst.

As there had been a wedding each year from 1935 to 1939, the other members of the family kept urging Pat not to break the sequence and to get married in 1940! At that time, no romance seemed imminent!

Pat was then at Monkton School, Dorset, acting as Secretary to the Dean Close boys who had been evacuated to Monkton School for the duration of the war. Andrew Hurst was on the Monkton School staff and he and Pat resided in the same school for some months. Later, when Andrew joined up, they decided to get married.

Pat wanted to get married in the Dean Close School Chapel. The difficulty was that the chapel was not licensed for weddings. To solve this, Pat and Andrew went to the Registry Office in the morning and were legally married. Pat handed her wedding ring back to Andrew and they had their religious marriage in the afternoon in the school chapel!

Of course, we were all pleased that she had not broken the sequence of six weddings in six consecutive years!

(To quote Pat: she did it with four months to spare!)

August 10th 1940 was a memorable day. It was the start of the Battle of Britain.

Dora and Alison (aged 6 months) were staying with Eric's parents in Oxford. Eric's father, Lt. Col Tucker, was one of the special cases allowed a car and they drove from Oxford to Cheltenham to attend the wedding. Eric joined them there in uniform from where his regiment was stationed at that time. As soon as the reception was over, they were anxious to get back to Oxford and be home in case the Invasion of Britain began!

Mercifully for all in Britain, it didn't happen, but the Battle of Britain in the air was fought that week and the weeks following.

In December 1939, soon after the outbreak of the war, Gillian Robertson was born in Edinburgh. By that time, Edwin had taken up his post as Professor of Obstetrics in Queen's College, Ontario, Canada. The Battle of the Atlantic had begun so it was an anxious time to sail to Canada. However, the Robertson family wished to be together, so Hannah and Gillian (aged 6 weeks) crossed safely to Canada where they remained on a permanent basis.

Jenny was already in S. Rhodesia with Jack, but it was not till 1948 that she was able to see her family in Britain again.

Hugo was looking after the interests of the evacuees of Dean Close School to Monkton Combe and also the Dean Close Prep School in Cheltenham. He tried to enlist in the army but was deeply disappointed to be told on medical grounds that he could not be accepted. He had previously had two abdominal operations.

During 1938, Eric joined the Belfast Branch of the Royal Corps of Signals. When war was declared in September 1939, he was immediately "called up". In November, he was posted to England and from there, was joined to the British Expeditionary Force and crossed to France. When France fell during the summer of 1940, thankfully, Eric's regiment was diverted from going to Dunkirk and was sent along the coast to Cherbourg. There they were told to set fire to their vehicles and to board the available ships. Actually, Eric was on the last ship that sailed for England and thankfully, they all docked there safely. For the next year, his Unit was posted in different parts of England – Harrow, Coventry, and Middlesbrough. Then, in August 1941, it was given Embarkation leave and sailed for an unknown destination some weeks later.

For the next three years, he was stationed in Persia and Iraq. One interesting happening was that his Signals Unit was in charge of all communications at the time of the meeting in Teheran of Churchill, Stalin and Roosevelt in August 1941.

On account of Mr Bing's health, he was allowed repatriation and was sent to Redford Barracks in Edinburgh to be at hand in case Mr Bing could not continue. He was finally "de-mobbed" in September 1945.

(Mr Bing was Headmaster/Owner of Rockport Prep School in N. Ire-land. Eric was assistant master there and was to take over as Head-master after Mr Bing. He suffered badly from an arthritic hip – no hip replacements in those days – and had to retire early. Eric and Dora took over Rockport in October 1945, with Alison aged five and Rosalind aged tenweeks. But that is another story!)

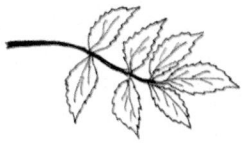

CHAPTER 14

Family Gatherings

Knockearn House today

"Withdraw thy foot lest thy neighbour be weary of thee". This is a phrase my mother often used when we were setting off to visit someone, fearful that someone would say, "I wish they hadn't stayed so long," and hopeful the hosts would comment "I wish they had stayed longer". In other words, don't outstay your welcome... On a weekend in July 1989, I don't think anyone would have outstayed their welcome. Such was the nature of that weekend. Buzzing with excitement was a large stone Victorian house set in the small spa town of Crieff in Perthshire, Scotland. Pilgrims – for it really was a pilgrimage – were travelling from as far afield as Australia, South Africa and Canada to join members of their extended family for a Reunion of 53 persons, ages ranging from a few months to the oldest at 86. The house, Knockearn (now a private house), was one of the boarding houses of Morrison's Academy and many years before had been the

home of the Reverend Peter Macainsh, the forefather of all those 53 individuals. In fact, the oldest members of the party, siblings, Hannah aged 86, Jenny aged 83, Dora aged 79 and Patricia aged 75, were all grandchildren of Peter Macainsh and had spent many happy holidays in Knockearn House as children.

Family Reunion, Crieff 1989

The small country town of Crieff was shining in the sun and the trees surrounding the house were in their full lush green summer plumage as people arrived to register. Names were checked on arrival in a hurly-burly of chattering and excitement and shrieks of joy as cousins, aunts and uncles greeted each other with hugs. Each family was allocated accommodation around the buildings of Morrison's Academy. The teenagers had great excitement trying to find their rooms, rushing here, there and everywhere. The oldest, delighted to be in the familiar house, and the youngest with parents were to stay in Knockearn and the rest were sent to school dormitories around Crieff where there was a mixture of dormitories and rooms which accommodated two persons. All meals were held in the Academy Hall (the school assembly hall) where the school caterers provided delicious food – even a fine celebration dinner on the Saturday night. Some members of the group happily took on various duties such as organising a golf tournament, a tennis tournament, the provision of booze, nursing care, the discipline and even a chaplain. During Saturday, people could choose any of the activities and some of the group decided to visit the nearby hamlet of Monzie where Peter Macainsh was born and where they studied with great interest the gravestones of our Macainsh ancestors. Everyone remarked on the longitude of the lives written on the stones!

Macainsh grave Monzie

The whole weekend was one of fun, laughter and harmony. The oldest members of the party took great delight in going down memory lane exploring the places they played in as children in the Knockearn garden – "here's the witches' hole", "do you remember the orchard?" The youngest group presented their own hilarious entertainment in the evening after the celebration dinner. Excellent speeches were delivered by Hannah Robertson, Martyn Hurst, Sonny Sadinsky, Hugh Elder and Carl Tams. (See family tree to see who they are). Fortunately, the weather was very kind and Crieff sparkled in the sunshine. The vivid green of the grass on the golf courses and around – a delight to those from Australia and Africa, and the hazy blue and purple of the hills surrounding the town all added to the thorough enjoyment of the weekend. Our only sadness was the fact that our mother was the only one of the sisters not there. She died of cancer at the age of 67. Her brother, Hugo, has also died, suffering from Parkinson's disease. They were greatly missed. Their sisters survived well into their nineties and one even made it to 103. Two cousins, Elspeth Robertson and Peter Elder, had died before their time (Elspeth in a car crash and Peter of cancer). One in-law, Jack Park, had passed away at the good age of 96. I'm sure their nearest felt the loss. The total number of surviving relations amounted to fifty-three all present in Crieff that weekend. The end of our jollities came on the Sunday afternoon, after a small service conducted by the Rev Gordon Tams, when we said our farewells – a poignant moment as we knew we would not see some of our dear relations, particularly the oldest members, again.

However, some of us were to meet again in 2002 with two of the surviving aunts and were delighted when our offspring expressed a wish to join us. The total number of relations this time was thirty-six. It was so amazing that all of us, with our different interests and lifestyles, should meet and have such harmonious weekends. We met in Crieff again – this time in the comfort of a hotel and not school dormitories. The value of families had always been impressed on us and it was here that we saw that in action. To have the support of all this extended family is a very remarkable experience. I believe it was after these events and having met the older generation that my daughter said, "Mum, I think you should write about the Aunts – they have lived through so many interesting times".

Elder Reunion, 1989

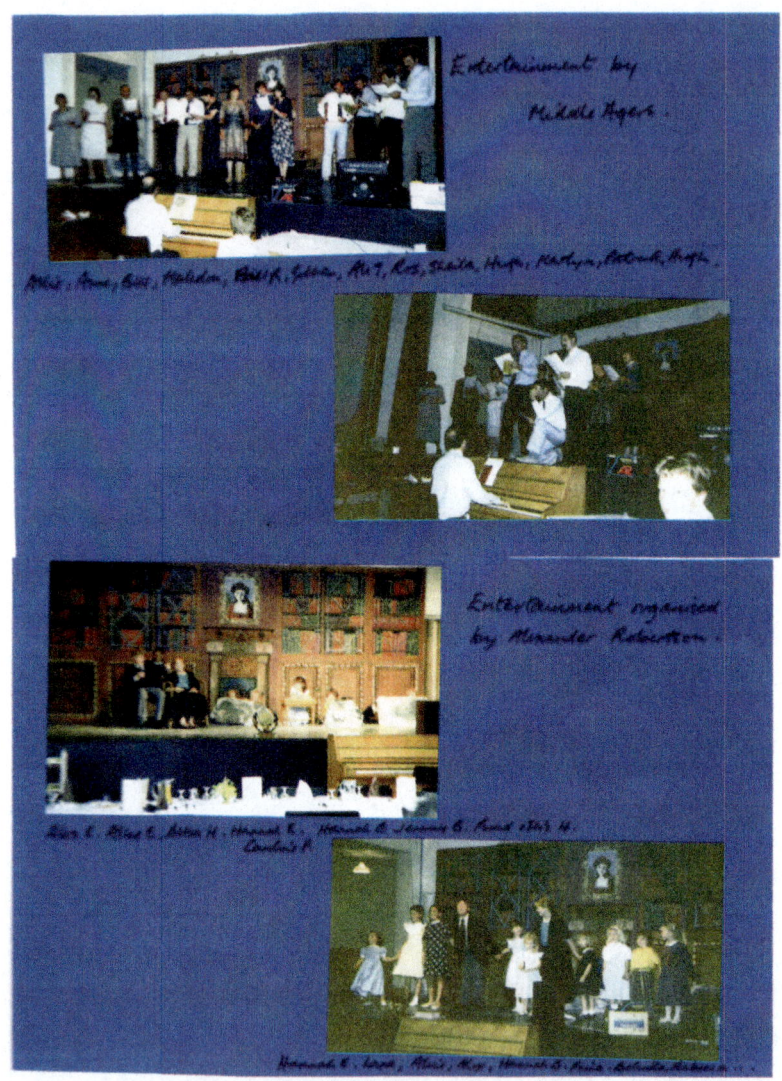

Elder Reunion, 1989

Second family reunion, Murraypark Hotel, Crieff 2002

We have told the story of the five aunts and their one brother. They have lived a privileged life but not without its sorrows. Families have suffered the tragedy of children dying, three in infancy, one aged 5 of cancer and another aged 24 killed in a road accident. They were deeply affected by this. Others have suffered difficult illnesses. (At present three members of the family suffer from Multiple Schlerosis). They have all brought courage, humour and joy into our lives.

CHAPTER 15

Great-Granny's Heirlooms

Hannah Gilbert Macainsh passed to her daughter, Hannah Elder, various interesting pieces of dress. These have been passed on to subsequent generations and it was Anne Bolam (the eldest offspring of our parents' children) who took most responsibility for them and sent them round the country when they were needed. The items include:

1. Three Victorian Dresses

One of the dresses was Hannah Gilbert's wedding dress. All the dresses now reside with Anne Bolam and we're hoping that some museum will take them. Alas, with the Pandemic, places have been closed recently and trying to place them has been put on hold. I was hoping to find a place in Crieff Museum – back to where it all began.

Sadly, I don't have a picture of the third dress.

Victorian dresses

2. The Wedding Veil

This veil, made of **Honiton** lace, has been worn by many brides over many years. Unfortunately, it is very fragile now and has become a creamy colour. It is over 100 years old. Not all brides want to wear something that is not pure white as it's often difficult to find a dress of the same colour. With families spreading out and many living abroad, it has not always been easy to get the veil to those who would like it.

Hugh and Hannah Elder

Elder-Macainsh wedding, 6 September 1900

Henry and Fiona Peterkins wedding with veil June 2006

The wedding veil originally belonged to **Mrs Graham Gilbert** who was married sometime between 1850 and 1900. She gave it to **Hannah Gilbert Macainsh** to wear at her wedding on 6th September 1900. Hannah Gilbert Macainsh married the Rev. Hugh Elder.

The following of her daughters wore the veil.

30th November 1935	Alison Anne Macainsh Elder married Dr George Alexander Grant Peterkin
31st July 1936	Dora Gilbert Elder married Eric John Gordon Tucker
3rd April 1937	Hannah Margaret Macainsh Elder married Dr Edwin Moody Robertson
10th August 1940	Vera Patricia Menzies Elder married Andrew William Hurst

The following of Hannah and Hugh Elder's grandchildren wore the veil

26th August 1966	Alison Gordon Tucker married Gordon Thomas Carl Tams
21st October 1967	Anne Margaret Grant Peterkin married David Bolam
1st May 1971	Alison Grant Peterkin married William Robert Agnew Logie
1st April 1972	Rosalind Dora Elder Tucker married Robert Douglas Arnold

The following of their Grandsons' brides wore the veil

24th August 1968	Victoria Carnegie married Conon William Grant Peterkin
14th May 1977	Penelope Kemp-Jones married Hugh Elder Hurst
25th February 1984	Jaqueline Joan Scarrisbrick married Andrew Patrick Hurst

The following of their great-grandchildren wore the veil

20th March 1993	Rosemary Grant Bolam married Kenneth James Aknai
	Granddaughter of Alison and Grant Peterkin and daughters of Anne and David Bolam
15th April 2000	Frances Anne Grant Bolam married Rory Patrick Neary
6th September 2003	Ailsa Patricia Hurst married Robert John Guidi
	(Granddaughter of Patricia and Andrew Hurst and daughter of Martyn and Sue Hurst)
20th September 2003	Hannah Margaret Alison Logie married Alexander Robertson.
	(Granddaughter of Alison and Grant Peterkin and daughter of Alison and Bill Logie)
June 2006	Henry Peterkin married Fiona Walker
	(Grandson of Alison and Grant Peterkin and son of Bill and Vicky Peterkin)

Other Brides in the family (who wore other veils or headwear)
Daughter of Hugh and Hannah Elder
Janet Isobel Elder married Jack Chalmers Park
Their wedding took place in South Africa   Mar 1938

Grandchildren of Hugh and Hannah Elder
Sharon Jackson married William Stead Robertson	31st May 1969
Gillian Mary Margaret Robertson married Stanley Sadinsky	7th December 1969
Susan Elizabeth Cliff married Martyn William Melford Hurst	7th March 1970
Helen Patricia Bouvert married Hugh John Mainwaring Elder	10th April 1976
Sheila Hannah Gordon Tucker married Reginald Arthur Bloom	24th August 1979
Diana Priday married Malcolm Chalmers Park	13th November 1984

Great-grandchildren of Hugh and Hannah Elder
Struan Robertson married Jennifer Alkenbrach	
Ellie Sadinsky married Peter Jeffrey	
Millie Sadinsky married John Cowden	
Lara Arnold married Robert Theakston	21st April 2003
Louise Peterkin married Stephen Leigh	21st August 2003
Claire Anderson married Jonathan Tams	20th November 2003
Duncan Robertson married Alison	20th August 2004
Robert Logie married Hannah Cockburn	27th July 2007

3. The Christening Robe

The Robe is also over 100 years old and is becoming quite fragile. The first baby to be christened was Hannah Gilbert Macainsh/Elder. Not so many babies are being christened these days so although many babies have worn it over the years, in the last century, very few have done so.

The following babies wore the robe at their Christenings

Hannah Gilbert Elder (nee Macainsh)	**1874**

Her Children

Hannah Margaret Macainsh Elder	1903
Hugh Elder	1905
Janet Isobel Elder	
Alison Anne Macainsh Elder	1907
Dora Gilbert Elder	1909
Vera Patricia Menzies Elder	1914

Her Grandchildren

Anne Margaret Grant Peterkin	1938 (baptised by her grandfather, Rev. Hugh Elder)
Gillian May Margaret Robertson	1939
Alison Gordon Tucker	1940
Alison Grant Peterkin	1940
Conon William Grant Peterkin	1942
Marty William Melford Hurst	1942
Rosalind Dora Elder Tucker	1945
Hugh Elder Hurst	1947

Sheila Hannah Gordon Tucker	1948
Andrew Patrick Hurst	1949

Her Great-Grandchildren

Karl Eric Gordon Tams	1968
Rosemary Grant Bolam	1970
Alistair Hugh Gordon Tams	1970
Louise Grant Peterkin	1972
Robert William Agnew Logie	1973
Simon Andrew Hurst	1973
Jonathan Gilbert Gordon Tams	1973
Hugh James Arnold	1974
Frances Anne Grant Bolam	1974
Henry Forest Grant Peterkin	1975
Hannah Margaret Alison Logie	1975
Philip James Gordon Tams	1975
Ailsa Patricia Hurst	1975
Alexander Grant Logie	1977
Lara May Louise Arnold	1980
Rebecca Louise Hurst	1985
Hannah Elizabeth Elder	1985
Fiona Kathleen Hurst	1986

Her Great-Great-Grandchildren

Charlotte Hannah Neary	2004
Madeleine Rose Elizabeth Guide	2006
Michael David Neary	2007
Isabella Linnea Arnold	2009
Gemma Christina May Arnold	2011
Charlotte Elizabeth Logie	2022

Descendants who did not wear the Christening Robe
Grandchildren

Catherine Hannah Chalmers Park	1938
Elspeth Hannah Robertson	1942
William Stead Robertson	1943
Malcolm Chalmers Park	1943
Hugh John Mainwaring Elder	1948
Peter Macainsh Elder	1952

Great-Grandchildren

Thomas William Grant Peterkin	1970
Lesley Margaret Haddon	1970
Elspeth Anna Sadinsky	1970
Emily Elder Sadinsky	1972
Struan Edwin Robertson	1973
Jackson Duncan Robertson	1975
Douglas George Arnold	1976
Alexander William Robertson	1978
Hannah Katherine Tucker Bloom	1982
Caroline Elisabeth Chalmers Park	1985
Jeremy James Eric Bloom	1985

Great-Great-Grandchildren

Bethany Grant Aknai	1999
Naomi Grant Aknai	2002
Amy Isobel Hurst	2003
Jemima Hurst	2005
Huxley Leigh	2005
Alison Elizabeth Robertson	2007
Samuel Thomas Theakston	2007

Pia Rose Arnold	2009
Katherine Robertson	2009
George Francis Theakston	2009
Harrison Ian Arnold	2010
Benjamin Robert Theakston	2011
Helen Robertson	2012
Etta Elder Arnold	2017

4. The Silver Teapot

Hugh Elder and teapot

This beautiful silver teapot was presented to Hugh and Hannah Elder by their congregation on the occasion of their marriage on 6th September 1900. It is now in the safe hands of Hugh Elder. We had the pleasure of partaking tea with him and Helen, his wife, and the teapot, all beautifully polished, was produced for tea on the terrace. It was accompanied by cucumber sandwiches and strawberries and sponge cake.

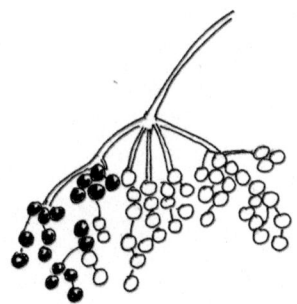

Epilogue

I believe that Aunts and Uncles are wonderful institutions. We, as a family, have been deeply blessed by being surrounded by loving and caring people; people who have always taken such an interest in us, welcomed us into their homes and given us a wonderful stability in our lives. They always made us feel valued. I hope we have in some ways given that to the next generation. The world is changing at a very fast rate, and families are changing too, with surrogacy and divorce creating new types of relationships. It is, therefore, more important than ever that the young are given that stability and feeling that they are valued. The values which we have inherited have been passed down through the generations from the Rev Peter Macainsh and Hannah, the Rev Hugh Elder and Hannah and our parents. It is with a great sense of gratitude that I conclude this story of the Elder family. We have sound, deep roots and a delightful variety of fruits.

The Aunts – Mary, Hugo's wife, Dora, Jenny, Hannah and Pat

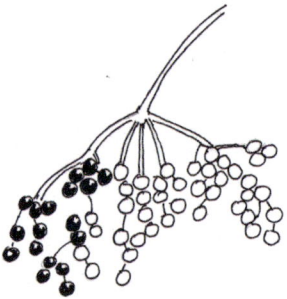

Appendix

Family Trees

1. Gilbert Macainsh Family Tree

THE GILBERT - MACAINSH FAMILY - TREE

Introduction

The document which I have called "The Gilbert-Macainsh Family-Tree" - preserved by my Mother with other family papers - is of great interest, but regrettably incomplete. Important dates are missing, and there are other omissions. For example, although the year of the marriage of 'The Progenitor' - the first JOHN GILBERT - is recorded (1758), the date of his birth is not, nor is the year of his death. Assuming that he married when he was in his twenties, he was born probably about 1730, and that year may serve as the starting-point of the Family-Tree; but it is only conjecture, not recorded fact. Another example is that the second JOHN GILBERT, younger son of the first, was married and had two daughters; but the name of his wife is not mentioned - a strange omission. These are only two examples of the incompleteness of the document: there are many others.

However, it is possible to set out what I shall call " A Line of Direct Descent " - from JOHN GILBERT of the early 18th Century to the junior members of the present generation of the family in the later part of the 20th Century - a span of about two-hundred and fifty years. This I have done, leaving out those branches of the family which are not relevant to the Line of Direct Descent, but including notes of information about individuals which should be of interest to all those who have in JOHN GILBERT a common ancestor.

May 1982   H. E.

Section I

<u>JOHN GILBERT</u> (born c.1730)   married   <u>CHRISTIAN McCOMISH</u>
1758

Children:
1. Andrew   born 1762   died 1838 – unmarried
2. Catherine   "   1765   "   ?   – married
3. Ann   "   1771   "   ?   – unmarried
4. John   "   1774   "   ?   – married

Notes:

The name of <u>Andrew</u> Gilbert is followed by the description
'of Yorkhill'. Presumably this was a residential property
of some importance, for it was passed on by inheritance and
carried the family name with it.

<u>Catherine</u> Gilbert is next in the 'line of direct descent'.
The name of her husband was Colin Macainsh: (see below).

The second <u>John</u> Gilbert was an officer of the Army with the
rank of Captain, and may have served in the Napoleonic War,
but there is no record of his service or even his regiment.
He was the original owner of the military dress-sword which
later belonged to my Grandfather and is now in my possession.
The date of his death is not known, but it must have preceded
the death of his brother Andrew, for he did not inherit the
property of Yorkhill, which passed to his elder daughter in
1838. The name of his wife is not recorded, but they had
two daughters – Jane and Cecilia. Both married, and their
husbands were both named Graham – they may have been brothers –
but there were no children of either marriage. Jane inherited
the family property from her uncle Andrew, and was then known
as Mrs. Graham Gilbert of Yorkhill. She died in 1877.
I remember being told by my mother that Mrs. Graham Gilbert
bequeathed to my Grandfather a substantial legacy, which enabled
him to retire in financial comfort, and subsequently made it
possible for my Mother to provide for her six children a
first-class education at school and university.

After the death of Mrs. Graham Gilbert in 1877, the family proper
was inherited by the eldest grand-daughter of Catherine (Gilbert)
Macainsh – Christina McCulloch, whose married name was Crerar.
She then became Mrs. Crerar Gilbert of Yorkhill. In due course
it passed to her son, Daniel; but there the record of ownership e
Presumably Yorkhill was sold and passed out of the family.

Section II

CATHERINE GILBERT (born 1765)   married COLIN MACAINSH
(Daughter of John Gilbert)   (date unknown)

Children: 1. Donald   born ? died ? – married
           2. Christian   "   ?   "   ? – married
           3. Margaret   "   ?   " 1869 – married
           4. Grace   "   ?   "   ? – married
           5. Helen   "   ?   " 1350 – married

Notes:

This Section is particularly unsatisfactory because
so few dates are recorded.

Donald Macainsh is next in the 'line of direct descent.'
The name of his wife was Ann Maclaren (see below)

Christian Macainsh married a man named James McCulloch,
and they had four daughters, the eldest of whom, Christina
Ann, inherited Yorkhill after the death of Mrs. Graham Gilbert
in 1877. (Christian herself had died before that year.)
Christina Ann McCulloch married a man named Crerar, and after
inheriting the estate she was known as Mrs. Crerar Gilbert.
The Crerar Gilberts had three children, a son and two daughters.
The son, Daniel, inherited Yorkhill – as already mentioned; but
apparently was its last owner of this family property.

Margaret Macainsh married a man named Duncan Maclaren, and
they had seven children, three sons and two daughters.
                                         Four.

Grace Macainsh married a man named Benjamin Taylor, and they
had two sons; but this branch of the family died out in the
next generation.

Helen Macainsh married a man named Stewart; but there were
no children of the marriage.

Section III

DONALD MACAINSH (born ?)   married   ANN MACLAREN
(Son of Catherine (Gilbert) Macainsh)   (date unknown)

Children: Twins - a boy and a girl: the girl lived for
            only a few weeks: the boy survived.
            1. Peter   born 1824   died 1913 - married.

Notes:

Although the dates of Donald's birth and marriage are not
known, it is certain that his death occurred before 1876,
for it is recorded that Ann Maclaren died in that year,
and she was then a widow. Donald, therefore, could not
have inherited the family property of Yorkhill, as it was
owned by Mrs. Graham Gilbert until 1877.

Donald lived at Monzie, near Crieff in Perthshire, which
was only a small village, although it had a Church - a
fact of some importance. Peter, the only child of Donald
and his wife, Ann, had a religious upbringing which led
him eventually to enter the Ministry. It is not known
what Donald's own occupation was, but probably he lived
in humble circumstances. Originally his son was apprenticed
to a tradesman in Crieff.

Donald's wife, Ann Maclaren, was a grand-daughter of
Peter Maclaren, whose wife was named Ann Menzies.
In the family burial-ground at Monzie there is a very
old grave-stone bearing the name of Menzies. My Mother
decided to revive that old family name for her youngest
child, who was baptised Vera Patricia Menzies Elder in
the year 1914.

Peter Macainsh is next in the 'line of direct descent'.

Section IV

PETER MACAINSH (born 1824)   married   HANNAH BROWN JOHNSTON
(Son of Donald Macainsh)   1871

One Child: Hannah Gilbert   born 1874 married 1900 died 1954.
              She is next in the 'line of direct descent.'

Notes:

Peter Macainsh, my Grandfather, married late, at the age of forty-seven,
and was fifty when his only child, my Mother, was born. His wife was
nine years younger.

It has been mentioned already that he was born and bred in the small
village of Monzie and was apprenticed to a tradesman of Crieff – an
ironmonger. Probably he served his term as an apprentice, but his
ambition was to become a Minister of the Gospel, and in 1849, at the
age of twenty-five, he became a student of the Free Church of Scotland's
Hall of Divinity in Edinburgh. Among the family papers is a certificate
issued by the Presbytery of Auchterarder – in which Monzie was situated
dated 1850 and stating that Mr. Peter Macainsh had been examined in
Hebrew, Greek, Latin and Theology to the entire satisfaction of the
Presbytery and would now proceed to the studies of the second year
at the Hall of Divinity. This suggests that at least part of the
cost of his training for the Ministry was provided by the Presbytery.
The course of studies of that first year was formidable for a young
man whose early education had been in a village school, and the
apprentice of Crieff must have used his spare-time well in preparing
for admission to the Hall of Divinity. In this task he certainly
had help and encouragement from the Minister of Monzie, who took
part in the service several years later at which Peter Macainsh
was ordained. This Minister, whose name was Ormond. may have been
a good scholar himself ready and willing to do what he could for
a promising young man in his parish.

By the year 1855 Peter Macainsh, not yet ordained, was living at
Lochgelly in Fife, licensed by the Presbytery of Kirkaldy to conduct
services of worship. There was no church then in the small town
of Lochgelly, which was only a 'Home Mission Station' of the
Presbytery; services were held in a local hall. However, there
was a growing demand that the Mission should become a 'Charge'
in its own right with an ordained Minister responsible for it.
In 1856 the Presbytery consented, and the Rev. Peter Macainsh
became the first Minister of Lochgelly, although there was not
yet an actual church-building. That came a year later, when
in 1857 a Church was built, paid for by private subscription.
Later it was named 'The Macainsh Church', to commemorate a
continuous ministry of thirty-five years.

Notes: (continued)

A copy has survived of an extract from The Fifeshire Advertiser of 18th October, 1856, which refers to the ordination service and the induction of the Rev.Peter Macainsh to the new 'Charge' of Lochgelly. There is also a copy of the minute of the Presbytery of Kirkaldy recording the ordination. The first of these is as follows:

"On Sabbath last, Mr. Macainsh of the Free Church in Lochgelly was introduced to his Charge by the Rev. Mr. Ormond, of Monzie. Mr. Ormond preached a singularly able and eloquent discourse from the words of John XVI - 24: " Ask and ye shall receive, that your joy may be full". In introducing Mr. Macainsh he stated that he had known him as a Sabbath School scholar, as a Sabbath School teacher and as a student, and that if his knowlege of him in these several spheres entitled him to speak with confidence of his attainments, he was warrented to speak this day. Intellectually, morally and spiritually he could say that Mr. Macainsh was well qualified to occupy the office which he held. He therefore would congratulate the members and the adherents of the Free Church Congregation of Lochgelly on their choice of a minister........ "

In 1891, The Rev. Peter Macainsh retired, at the age of sixty-seven, from the Church of Lochgelly, of which he had been Minister for 35 years. He returned to his native county of Perthshire, and having by this time inherited a legacy from Mrs. Graham Gilbert, he built a house in Crieff for his retirement, named 'Knockearn'. Later he enlarged it in order to accommodate his grandchildren when they visited him – as they did regularly during school holidays. For many years 'Knockearn' was a second home for my sisters and myself.

In 1906 The Rev. Peter Macainsh celebrated the Golden Jubilee of his ordination, though the state of his health did not permit him to go to Lochgelly for the occasion. He was represented by his daughter and her husband, The Rev. Hugh Elder, who spoke on his behalf.

He died in 1913, in his eighty-ninth year. His widow, my Grandmother, died in 1919,aged eighty-six. They were both buried in the Churchyard of Monzie, beside the graves of his parents.

Section VI   ' THE   LINE   OF   DIRECT   DESCENT '

Summary

1st Generation.	JOHN GILBERT	born c.1730 ?
2nd Generation.	CATHERINE GILBERT * MACAINSH (Daughter of John Gilbert)	born 1765
3rd Generation.	DONALD MACAINSH (Son of Catherine Gilbert Macainsh)	born c.1789 ?
4th Generation	PETER MACAINSH (Son of Donald Macainsh)	born 1824
5th Generation.	HANNAH GILBERT MACAINSH * ELDER (Daughter of Peter Macainsh)	born 1874
6th Generation.	Children of Hannah Gilbert Macainsh Elder	born 1903 - 1914
7th Generation.	Grandchildren of the same.	born 1938 - 1951
8th Generation.	Great-Grandchildren of the same.	born 1968 onwards

Section VII   THE MACAINSH - ELDER FAMILY
              The Children of the Rev. Hugh Elder and his wife,
              Hannah Gilbert Macainsh: and their Descendants
                        - to the year 1982 -

              ------

1. <u>HANNAH MARGARET MACAINSH ELDER</u> married <u>Dr. EDWIN MOODY ROBERTSON</u>
        (born 1903)   1937

    <u>Children:</u> (i)   Gillian Mary Margaret   born 1939: married.
              (ii) Elspeth Hannah   born 1942: unmarried: died 1966.
              (iii) William Stead   born 1943: married.

<u>Note:</u>

<u>Hannah Elder</u> graduated in Medicine at Edinburgh University, and
practised as a Doctor for several years before her marriage.
In 1939, her husband, also an Edinburgh graduate, was appointed
Professor of Gynaecology at Queen's University, Kingston, Ontario,
Canada. The Robertsons settled permanently in that country.

(i) <u>GILLIAN MARY MARGARET ROBERTSON</u> married <u>STANLEY SADINSKY</u>
        (born 1939)   1969

    <u>Children:</u> a. Elspeth Anna   born 1970
              b. Emily Elder   born 1972

(iii) <u>WILLIAM STEAD ROBERTSON</u> married <u>SHARON LYNNE JACKSON</u>
        (born 1943)   1969

    <u>Children:</u> c. Struan Edwin   born 1973
              d. Jackson Duncan   born 1975
              e. Alexander William   born 1978

<u>Notes:</u>

Gillian Robertson, before her marriage, worked as a journalist
and broadcaster.
Her husband's family was originally Russian.

William Robertson qualified as a Lawyer and practised in Toronto.

------

tes: Gillian Robertson graduated from Queens University and then
obtained the Harvard-Radcliffe Certification in Business Administration
in Boston. Both before and after her marriage she worked as a journalist
and broadcaster. Her husband, whose family is originally from Russia,
is a Professor of Law at Queens University and a Q.C.
     Elspeth trained as a nurse at the Royal Victoria Hospital,Montreal,
and obtained her diploma of Nursing Science at Queens University. At the
time of her death in a car accident, she was a clinical instructor at
the Sick Childrens Hospital, Toronto.
     William obtained his undergraduate degree from Acadia University,

Elder: Roots and Fruits

Section VII (continued)   The Macainsh-Elder Family

2.   HUGH ELDER   married   WINIFRED MARY STAGG
(born 1905)   1939

Children: (i) Hugh John Mainwaring   born 1948: married.
(ii) Peter Macainsh   born 1951: died 1956

Note: Hugh Elder, after graduating in Classical studies at
the Universities of Edinburgh and Oxford, became a
schoolmaster. He was an assistant master at Sherborne
School in Dorset for six years, and at Fettes College
in Edinburgh for three years. In 1938 he was appointed
Headmaster of Dean Close School, Cheltenham, where he
spent the War-years. In 1939 he married Mary Stagg,
daughter of Colonel M. Stagg, C.B.E., Royal Engineers.
In 1946 he was appointed Headmaster of Merchant Taylors'
School, Northwood, Middlesex, where he served until
his retirement in 1965. He and his wife went to live
in Somerset, and for the next ten years he worked as
a part-time Tutor in Classics at Millfield School.

(i) HUGH JOHN MAINWARING ELDER married HELEN PATRICIA BOUVERAT
(born 1948)   1976

Children: a. Alice Rose   born 1978

Note: Hugh John Elder, like his father and grandfather,
was a graduate of Edinburgh University, where he
read for the degree of LL.B. He then qualified
as a Solicitor in England, studying at Bristol
for the examinations of the Law Society. He
worked in London for three Firms of Lawyers in
succession and became a partner in the third
of these.

Section VII (continued)   The Macainsh-Elder Family

4. ALISON ANN MACAINSH ELDER married Dr. GEORGE ALEXANDER GRANT PETERKIN
       (born 1908)   1935

    Children: (i)   Anne Margaret Grant   born 1938: married
              (ii)   Alison Grant   born 1940: married
              (iii) Conon William Grant   born 1942: married

    Note: Alison Elder trained as a teacher of music, qualified L.R.A.M.,
           and taught piano-playing to private pupils before her marriage.
           Her husband, an Edinburgh University graduate in Medicine,
           practised as a Dermatologist before and after the War, in
           which he served abroad with the RAMC. Of the Elder children,
           Alison was the only one who remained resident in Edinburgh.
           She died in 1974, after suffering a stroke, aged sixty-five.

(i)   ANNE MARGARET GRANT PETERKIN married DAVID BOLAM
           (born 1938)   1967

       Children: a. Rosemary Grant   born 1970
                  b. Frances Anne Grant   born 1973

(ii)   ALISON GRANT PETERKIN married WILLIAM ROBERT AGNEW LOGIE
           (born 1940)   1971

       Children: c. Robert William Agnew   born 1973
                  d. Hannah Margaret Agnew   born 1975
                  e. Alexander Grant Agnew   born 1977

(iii) CONON WILLIAM GRANT PETERKIN married VICTORIA FORREST CARNEGIE
           (born 1942)   1968

       Children: f. Thomas William Grant   born 1970
                  g. Louise Grant   born 1972
                  h. Henry Forrest Grant   born 1974

    Notes: Before her marriage, Anne Peterkin qualified as a member
            of Princess Mary's R.A.F. Nursing Service. While serving
            as a Nurse, she met David Bolam who was a Dental Surgeon
            with the Royal Air Force.

            Alison Peterkin graduated at Edinburgh University, took a
            Diploma of Education at Cambridge, spent a year in Kenya
            on V.S.O. and had several teaching posts in the U.K.

            Conon William Peterkin graduated in Medicine at Edinburgh
            and became a General Practitioner in Forfar, where his
            Grandfather had also been a Doctor.

Elder: Roots and Fruits

Section VII (continued)   The Macainsh-Elder Family

5. DORA GILBERT ELDER married ERIC JOHN GORDON TUCKER
    (born 1910)   1936

    Children: (i)   Alison Gordon   born 1940: married.
              (ii) Rosalind Dora Elder   born 1945: married.
              (iii) Sheila Hannah Gordon   born 1948: married.

    Note: At the time of her marriage, Dora Elder was living with
          her parents at Moffat. Her husband, Eric Tucker, was
          Junior Partner of a privately-owned Preparatory school
          for boys in Northern Ireland – Rockport, Craigavad.
          Because of the War, in which he served with the Army
          abroad, his succession to the Headmastership was delayed
          until 1945; but in that year the Tuckers took over the
          management of the school. They remained in charge of it
          for twenty-nine years; having converted it into an
          Educational Trust, retired in 1974, and continued to
          live in the neighbourhood.

  (i) ALISON GORDON TUCKER married GORDON THOMAS CARL TAMS
      (born 1940)   1966

      Children: a. Carl Eric Gordon   born 1968
                b. Alastair Hugh Gordon   born 1970
                c. Jonathan Gordon   born 1973
                d. Philip James Gordon   born 1975

  (ii) ROSALIND DORA ELDER TUCKER married ROBERT DOUGLAS ARNOLD
       (born 1945)   1972

       Children: e. Hugh James   born 1974
                 f. Douglas George   born 1976
                 g. Lara May Louise   born 1980

  (iii) SHEILA HANNAH GORDON TUCKER married REGINALD ARTHUR BLOOM
        (born 1948)   1979

    Notes: Alison Tucker was a graduate of Queen's University, Belfast,
           took an Educational Diploma, and taught in several schools
           before her marriage.
           Rosalind Tucker also trained as a teacher and taught, both
           in the U.K. and in Kenya.
           Sheila Tucker, a graduate of Trinity College Dublin, held
           executive posts with Music International, and the Observer.

Section VII (continued) The Macainsh-Elder Family

7. VERA PATRICIA MENZIES ELDER married ANDREW WILLIAM HURST
       (born 1914)   1940

    Children: (i)   Martyn William Melford   born 1942: married
              (ii) Hugh Elder   born 1947: married
              (iii) Andrew Patrick   born 1949: unmarried.

    Note: Patricia Elder, a graduate of Edinburgh University, trained
            as a secretary and worked in London. In 1938 she joined her
            brother, then unmarried, as his hostess in the Headmaster's
            House of Dean Close School, Cheltenham. On the outbreak of
            War in 1939 its buildings were requisitioned, and a temporary
            alliance was formed with Monkton Combe School, where Andrew
            Hurst was an assistant master. He and Patricia were married
            in the following year, but by that time he was serving as
            an officer of the Army. When the War ended, after a brief
            return to teaching, he was appointed Assistant Director of
            Education for Buckinghamshire, and the Hursts settled in
            Amersham. Later on Patricia, having brought up her family,
            made a new career for herself as a teacher of handicapped
            children with the County L.E.A.

    (i)   MARTYN WILLIAM MELFORD HURST married SUSAN ELIZABETH CLIFF
           (born 1942)   1970

          Children: a. Simon Andrew   born 1973
                     b. Ailsa Patricia   born 1975
                     c. Belinda Elspeth Sarah   born 1977

    (ii) HUGH ELDER HURST married PENELOPE KEMP-JONES
           (born 1947)   1977

    Notes: Martyn Hurst was a graduate of Oxford University in
            Engineering - (a member of Merton College, where
            his father had been) - and subsequently was commissioned
            in the Royal Air Force. He served both in the U.K. and
            in Germany: in 1982 he had the rank of Wing Commander.
            Hugh Hurst was a graduate of St. Andrews University, and
            then qualified as a Solicitor: he practised in London.
            Patrick Hurst, a Chartered Accountant, worked in the
            field of Commerce.

2. The Elder Family Tree

Peter and Hannah MaCainsh built 'Knockearn' in Crieff in 1891.
(Peter Macainsh died Feb 17 1913; Hannah Macainsh died Aug 5 1919

Knockearn House, Crieff

Their only child, **Hannah** married **Hugh Elder** on
6 September 1900

Hannah and Hugh Elder

164

Hugh and Hannah Elder had **seven** children
Hugh Elder died July 11 1950; Hannah Gilbert Elder died Sept 1, 1954)

Hannah, Hugh (Hugo), Janet (Jenny), Alison, Dora, Peter (died in infancy Feb 6 1912) and Patricia

The following families are their grandchildren, great-grandchildren, great-great-grandchildren and great-great-great-grandchildren

The Robertson Family

Hannah (born Jan 20 1903 – died May 1998) married Edwin Robertson (died July 1977)

1. Baby boy born and died June 15 1938

2. Gillian (Born Dec 4 1939) married **Stanley (Sonny)** Sadinsky Dec 7 1969
    a. Elspeth (born Nov 30 1970) married Peter Jeffery Sept 20 1997
      i)   Spencer George Sadinsky born 2001
      ii) Grayson Nathanial Sadinsky born 2004
    b. Millie (born Dec 12 1972) married John Cowden Sept 8 2001
      i) Benjamin William Avery (born 2002)

    ii) Max Elder (born 2005)

    iii) Elliott Duncan (born 2008)

3. **Elspeth** (born March 13 1942 – died Nov 11 1966 (in road accident)

4. **William** (born 1943) married **Sharon (Sherri)** Jackson May 31 1969

    a. Struan (born 1973) married Jennifer Alkenbrack July 8 2000

        i) Jackson Connor (born 2002)

        ii) Molly Olivia (born 2003)

        iii) Aidan William Douglas (born 2007)

    b. Jackson Duncan (born Sept 20 1975) married Alison Parker Sept 8 2004

        i) Kaiya Hannah (born 2006)

        ii) Crew Parker (born 2009)

        iii) Beckett Duncan (born 2013)

    c. Alexander (born 1978) partner Murray Daniel Henderson 1978

        i) Edwin Gage Henderson 2020

The Elder Family

Hugh (Hugo) (Born 26 Feb 1905 – Died 5 Feb 1986) married Dec 1939 Mary Stagg (Born 1 March – Died 3 August 1998)

1. **Hugh** (born Aug 1948) married **Helen** Bouverat Apr 1976
   a. Alice Rose (born Oct.1978) married James Oliver Peter Bishop 10 Sept 2005
      i) Tobias Hugh William (born 2010)
      ii) Henrietta Rose Mary (born 2013)
   b. Hannah Jane (born 12 Oct 1985) married Richard Douglas Yates9 May 2015
      i) Douglas Henry William (born 2017)
      ii) Eve Mabel Yates (born 2019)

2. **Peter** (born June 1951 – died 1956 (cancer))

The Park Family

Janet (Jenny) (Born 9 Mar 1906 – Died Feb 2003) married March 1938 Jack Chalmers Park (Born 1893 – Died June 1989)

1. **Catherine** (born Dec 1938) married **Bryan** Haddon Apr 1966
   a. Lesley (born June 1970) married X Andrew Terwin Apr 1999
      married Anton Martyn Apr 2015
      i) Cameron George (born Apr 2001)

    b.   Ian (born Dec 1971) married Julia Horne 2004

        i)   Carmen Olivia (born 2010)

        ii) Paige Skye (born 2016)

2. **John (**born and died Oct 1941)

-

3. **Malcolm** (born 1943) married Nov 1982 **Diana** Pridey (died Sept 2002)

    a.   Caroline (born 1983) married Shannon McKrill Jan 2012

        i)   Grace Diana (born 2016)

        ii) Ella (born 2019)

    b.   Lara born 1970 married Michael Bryan1995

        i)   Anthony and Mikaela, twins (born 1996)

            Mikaela married Graydon Ilderton 2013

        ii) Jordan (born 2012)

The Peterkin Family

Alison (Born 1907 – Died 1974) married Grant Peterkin Died 1987

1. **Anne** (born 15 June 1938) married 24 Oct 1967 **David** Bolam died September 2017

    a.   Rosemary (born 1970) married 1993 Kenneth Aknai Bethany (born 1999)married Joseph Hetherington 2023 Naomi (born 2002)

    b.   Frances (born 1973) married Rory Neary Apr 2000

(i) Charlotte Hannah (born 2004)

(ii)Michael David born 2007

2. Alison (born 1940) married **William (Bill)** Logie May 1971

    a.   Robert (born Jan 1973) married Hannah Cockburn July 2007

i)Hannah Beatrix Cockburn (born 2013)

ii)Penelope India Cockburn (born 2018)

    b.   Hannah (born July 1975) married Alex Robertson Sept 2003

(i)Alison Elizabeth (born 2006)

(ii) Katherine Susan (born 22 2008)

iii) Twins Helen and Douglas (born 2012)

    c.   Alexander (born 1977) married Cassie Black 14 Nov 2020

i) Charlotte Elizabeth (born 2022)

3. William (Bill) m. Aug. 1968 Victoria Carnegie

    a.   Thomas (born Apr 1970) married Sinead Mackay Feb 2014

        i)   Iris Rose (born 2015)

        ii) Hugh William born 2017

    b.   Louise (born May 1972) married Stephen Leigh Aug 2003

        i)   Huxley Forrest (born 2005)

        ii) Theodore Morris (born 2007)

    c.   Henry (born June 1974) married Fiona Walker June 2006

        i)   Libby (born 2008)

        ii) Madeleine (born 2010)

The Tucker Family

Dora (Born Oct 1909 – Died 2013) married July 1936 Eric Tucker Died 1996

1. **Alison** (born Jan 1940) married Aug 1966 **Gordon** Tams died 27th March 2014 *Please complete the data on this family*
   a. Carl (born Oct 1968) married Fiona Downey June 2008
      i) Tommie James Gordon born 2012
   b. Alastair (born June 1970) partner Julie
   c. Jonathan (born Aug 1973) married Claire Anderson Nov 2003
      i) Louis Joshua (born J 2005)
      ii) Evie Freya (born 2012)
   d. Philip (born Dec 1975) married Kate Krawcsyk 2019
      i) Alfie Rex Keltie (born 1998)
      ii) Antek born 2005
      iii) Adam born 2011

2. **Rosalind** (born 1945) married **Robert (Bob)** Arnold Apr 1972
   a. Hugh (born Jun 1974) married Camilla Birch 2006
      i) Isabella born2009
      ii) Gemma born 2011
   b. Douglas (born Jun 1976) married Helen Greig
      i) Pia Rose born 2007
      ii) Harrison Ian born 2010
      iii) Etta born 2017

   c. Lara (born Jun 1980) married Robert Theakston
March 2003
- i) Samuel Thomas born 2007
- ii) George Francis born 2009
- iii) Benjamin born 2011

3. **Sheila** (born Mar 1948 died June 16) married **Reginald (Reg)** Bloom Aug 1979
   a. Hannah (born Nov 1982) partner Damien Brian Aldred (born 1979)
   b. Jeremy (born Mar 1985) married Rochelle Elizabeth Aug 2013
- i) Harrison James (born 2014)
- ii) Oliver Tucker (born 2016)
- iii) Charles Raymond (born 2016)
- iv) Archer Reginald (born 2021)

The Hurst Family

Patricia (Born 12 Jan 1914 – Died 29/7/2004X) married 10 Aug 1940 Andrew Hurstdied 27/7/2012X (*Please complete data*)

1. **MARTYN** (born 2 Sept 1942) married 10 Mar 1970 **Susan** Cliff died 14 October 2018
   a. Simon (born 5 June 1973) married Melissa Buckingham 7 Mar 2001
- i) Amy (born 2002)
- ii) Jemima (born 2004)

b. Ailsa (born 7 Apr 1975) married Robert Guidi 6 Sept 2003
  i) Madeleine (born 2005)
  ii) William (born 2008)
  iii) Anabelle (born 2014)
c. Belinda (born 1977) partner Richard Scarisbrook
  i) Octavia (born 2016)

2. **Hugh** (born Feb 1947) married **Penelope** Kemp-Jones May 1977
  a. Elizabeth (born Apr 1984) married Casey High
    i) Russell Anthony 2020
    ii) Tobias born 2010
  b. Fiona (born Aug 1986) married Sam Maynard 2016
    i) Jack born 2019
    ii) George born 2022

3. **Patrick** (born May 1949) married Feb 1984 **Jacquiline** Scarisbrick died 1995
  a. Rebecca (born Aug 1985) married Hugh Dugdale 2012
    i) Florence Joan born 2014
    ii) Eleanor (Nelly) Dorothy born 2016
  b. William (born Sept 1988) married Emma Pybus 2021
  c. James (born 1990)

3. Hugh Elder's Family from Haddington

Hugh Elder's family (circa 1896)
Standing: William (doctor), George (doctor), John (lawyer)
Seated: Jane Hugh, Hugh (minister), Tom (farmer), James (farmer –
Athelstaneford)

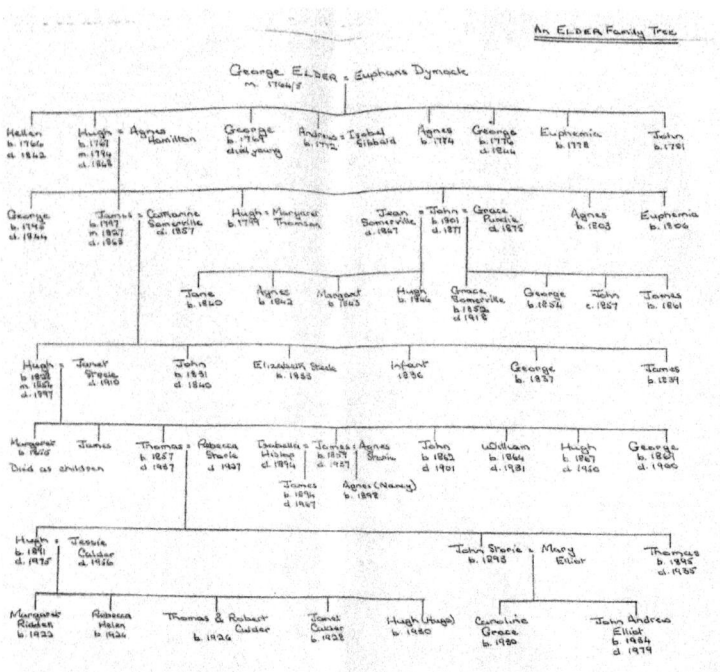

4. Extract from The Sentinel July 1917 from the Rev Hugh Elder, M.A.

Minister of Stockbridge Church 1910 – 1931
With the Y.M.C.A in France. Sunday at the Front

It is a beautiful Sunday morning – a perfect May day, though May has not yet come. The sun shines brilliantly in an almost cloudless sky. The guns, which last night were rending the heavens like thunder and lightning, are silent for a time as if Sabbath calm has fallen on them. As I go about the duties of the day in one hut preparing for the comfort of "the boys" of whom there are many here at present, two parade services are proceeding, one in the other hut, one in the open air.

Through the open door and window there falls upon the ear that great hymn of adoration "All hail the power of Jesus' name" sung by one congregation as only a body of men can sing it. "Crown him Lord of all". What visions and aspirations these words inspire of the time foreseen by the seer, when the Kingdom of the World shall become the Kingdom of our Lord and of his Christ and He shall reign for ever and ever. There follows from the other congregation "O Love that wilt not let me go". Amid so much that is loveless in this land of war – and not far from the place of meeting there are painful evidences of it – it is good to hear men assure their hearts of the love that never fails but holds men everywhere. "I lay in dust life's glory dead". Alas! Of how many of these fine men must that perforce be true before this war is finished? For them, how uplifting the hope "And from the ground there blossoms red, life that shall endless be".

Presently yet another note is struck – "Fight the good fight" – by men who have been in the trenches and who will soon be in the trenches again. "Lift up thine eyes and seek His face" they sing. That is the great source of courage and strength – the face of Jesus, the great Captain of Salvation. Comrades of the Navy and the Merchant Navy of remembered in "Eternal Father strong to save" – a favourite hymn with the land forces; and with Watt's great hymn of faith and consecration – "When I survey the wondrous Cross" the service in the open air ends.

"Were the whole realm of nature mine,
That were an offering far too small
Love so amazing, so divine,
Demands my soul, my life, my all."

So these men who have not counted their lives dear unto themselves and are in daily jeopardy in the high places of the field, consecrate themselves to their great and costly sacrifice in the cause of righteousness and liberty.

Presently, there ring out the words of command "Right dress" "Form Fours" "Quick March" and the men are off to their several tasks. Soon the booming of the big guns is heard not very far away.

I heard not one word of prayer or preaching in either service, but the praise of the boys greatly refreshed my soul and helped me to serve them in things temporal and spiritual.

In the afternoon, the present staff of the Brotherhood being all three Scots, we gave a free tea to all Scots who could attend. Sixty-three accepted our invitation. We sang the 100th Psalm and asked a blessing then gave the boys a real good tea. That finished, we asked them from whence they came and the name of their regiments. They came from 35 different places, from Inverness in the north to Stranraer in the south and from Kirkcaldy in the east to Ayr in the west and they belonged to 12 different regiments. Several were from Edinburgh, but none were Royal Scots and none were from Stockbridge. I gave them a short word on the Cross of St Andrew with its message of sacrifice, its sacrifice and ours – and we closed with the 2nd Paraphrase. So it was a real Scottish gathering.

LIFE BEHIND THE LINES

When the wagons and guns had been unhooked, the horses watered, tethered and fed, the boys made straight for our Hut, hungry, thirsty, anxious for a smoke and glad of the opportunity of resting and writing home to their friends. From 6 to 9, we were all at it, three workers and four orderlies, as hard as we could, to serve the men with tea, cocoa, tobacco, chocolate, paper, envelopes, etc. There was a little lull about 8 o'clock and we paused as usual for 10 minutes for worship. We are reading at present from a little Y.M.C.A. booklet entitled "Active Service" and the readings that evening were on "The Soldier's Victory". They included such texts as these:

"We are more than conquerors through Him that loved us"

"Thanks be unto God who giveth us the victory through our Lord Jesus Christ"

"The Eternal as thy Refuge and underneath are the everlasting arms and he shall thrust out thine enemies from before thee".

....

They had been in action off and on since January and had had a very rough time. They were most grateful for our attention to them and told us ours was the best place they had struck yet and assured us that they would never forget us. At long last, they took their departure. With "Goodnight", "Good luck", "God bless you, boys", we bade them adieu and went off to our billets very tired but very happy with the joy of service. To me, it was one of the nights of my life.

DOMESTIC ECONOMY

We have been engaged in the unromantic but necessary business of house-cleaning. This Hut has been open for about 18 months and was showing signs of tear and wear, besides being somewhat dirty after the traffic of the winter, when the mud here is indescribable. We have re-covered the counters and tables and decorated the walls and roof in a colour scheme of red, white and blue – with the result that we have transformed the appearance of the Hut and made it the object of admiration by all who have seen it, including many officers of high rank. We have stamped it as a Scottish Hut, by placing a magnificent Scottish Standard, the Lion Rampant, on the end wall, away from the counter and we have stamped it as a Brotherhood Hut, by putting the Brotherhood motto, "One if your Master, even Christ and all ye are brethren" on the wall, under a board which sets forth that the Hut is the gift of the Scottish Brotherhood. This is placed so as to catch the eyes of men as they enter the Hut, and constantly conveys its own message of allegiance and love. Our work goes on, on the usual lines, serving in the canteen, talking to the men, conducting worship every evening, and services on Sunday and Wednesday evenings. Also, we are cultivating the ground about the Hut, and have a vegetable garden on one side, and flower garden on the other.

RELIGIOUS OUTLOOK

There is no sign of a general revival of religion, but we have a good deal to encourage us. The distinctive feature of our religious work is a meeting for prayer after the Sunday evening service, started at the request of some of the boys themselves and in which they take part. Their prayers are touching at times in their simplicity and reality. Pray for us that we may make the most of our opportunity.

(These are extracts taken from letters sent to the Congregation at regular intervals to inform them of his work as a Y.M.C.A. Chaplain)

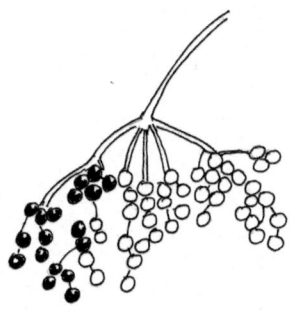

5. THE ELDER REUNION 1989

<u>PROGRAMME OF EVENTS FOR JULY 21st - 23rd.1989.</u>

Friday 21st July. -   From 2 pm families assemble at Knockearn House.
                      Tea and settle in.
                      7.00 - 8.00 DINNER in Academy Hall.
                      General chat and games for the children.

Saturday 22nd July - 8.30 - 9.30. BREAKFAST in Academy Hall.
                      Morning: Golf tournament at Glenalmond for any
                      one who wishes to 'have a go'.
                      1.00 - 2.00. LUNCH in Academy Hall.
                      2.30 - 4.00. Tennis tournament for
                      trouts,minnows and amoebas.
                      5.30 - 6.30. PHOTO-CALL at Knockearn House.
                      6.30 - 7.00. Drinks at Academy Hall.

                      7.00 - 9.00. GRAND CELEBRATION DINNER at
                      Academy Hall.

                      9.00 - 11.30. ENTERTAINMENT. Singing,
                      dancing,piping,fiddling, comic sketches by the
                      guests.

Sunday 23rd July -   8.30 - 9.30. Breakfast in Academy Hall.
                      10.00-10.20. Short service in Knockearn House
                                   drawing room.
                      10.30-11.00. Memories of the Moffat Manse by
                      Eric Tucker.

                      Morning : People are free to attend the above
                      or to take the opportunity to explore the area.
                      Macainsh graves can be seen in the graveyard at
                      Monzie Church - a very pretty little place a
                      few miles north of Crieff.

                      11.00 - 1.00. Cousin Archie, Cousin Helen
                                   Cousin Peggy and Sheena Peterkin
                      will appear for coffee and lunch.

                      1.00 -2.00. LUNCH.

                      Afternoon: families disperse.

Programme of events at Reunion

ROOM ALLOCATION

ADULTS   ROOM NUMBER

Hannah Robertson...1
Jenny Park..1

Mary Elder..8
Dora and Eric Tucker..5
Pat and Andrew Hurst 6
Gillian and Sonny Sadinsky..................................B

Bill and Sheri Robertson....................................G
Hugh, Helen and Hannah Elder................................4
Anne and David Bolam..A
Alison and Bill Logie.......................................M
Bill and Vicky Peterkin.....................................K
Alison and Gordon Tams ....F
Rosalind and Bob Arnold.....................................C
Shiela,Reg, and Jeremy Bloom 7
Martyn and Sue Hurst ....H
Hugh,Penny,Elizabeth and Fiona Hurst 2
Patrick,Jackie,Rebecca and William Hurst 3
Malcolm and Diana Park L

OFFSPRING

DORMITORY I   Millie,Ellie,Rosie,Louise,Lara Park.

Dormitory J   Carl,Alastair,Tom,Struan,Simon,Robert,Jonathan.

Dormitory D   Frances,Hannah Logie,Ailsa,Belinda,Alice.

Dormitory E   Henry,Hugh,Duncan, Philip.Douglas,
                Alexander L. Alexander R.

Dormitory 9   Lara Arnold,Hannah Bloom, Caroline Park.

NUMBERS are in KNOCKEARN HOUSE
LETTERS are in ACADEMY HOUSE   SEE MAPS OVERLEAF.......

Room allocation 1989 Reunion

181

MEMBERS OF CLAN ATTENDING REUNION	SPOUSE

(In chronological order)

Year	Member	Spouse
1903	Hannah Robertson	
1906	Jenny Park	
1909	Dora Tucker	Eric
1914	Patricia Hurst	Andrew
1919		Mary Elder
1938	Anne Bolam	David
1938	Catherine Park	
1939	Gillian Sadinsky	Sonny
1940	Alison Logie	Bill
1940	Alison Tams	Gordon
1942	Bill Peterkin	Vicky
1942	Martyn Hurst	Sue
1943	Bill Robertson	Sheri
1943	Malcolm Park	Diana
1945	Rosalind Arnold	Bob
1947	Hugh Hurst	Penny
1948	Hugh Elder	Helen
1948	Shiela Bloom	Reg
1949	Patrick Hurst	Jacquiline
1968	Carl Tams	
1970	Tom Peterkin	
	Rosemary Bolam	
	Elspeth Sadinsky	
	Alastair Tams	
1972	Louise Peterkin	
	Emily Sadinsky	
1973	Struan Robertson	
	Robert Logie	
	Frances Bolam	
	Jonathan Tams	
	Simon Hurst	
1974	Henry Peterkin	
	Hugh Arnold	
1975	Duncan Robertson	
	Hannah Logie	
	Philip Tams	
	Ailsa Hurst	
1976	Douglas Arnold	
1977	Alexander Logie	
	Belinda Hurst	
1978	Alexander Robertson	
	Alice Elder	
1980	Lara Arnold	
1982	Hannah Bloom	
1983	Caroline Park	
1984	Elizabeth Hurst	
1985	Rebecca Hurst	
	Jeremy Bloom	
	Hannah Elder	
1986	Fiona Hurst	
1988	William Hurst	

Elder Reunion 1989 Attendees

rds the offenders.
veral residents told the rald" this week that the slum has been growing in nt months, with rowdyism at worst on Friday and Saturday its.

t's getting dangerous," said David Millar "People barred a local pubs somehow get aselves well oiled, and fight, nt obscenities, urinate even nst doors and vandalise the . And the police never seem ift anyone.

The latest incident last week an eventual police presence e I'd given up trying to get ugh to the local station and Perth HQ. But again, it was a question of 'On your way, and frankly it's not enough

After the police went on their the youths were straight back t. Something's got to be done re innocent people get hurt. re are pensioners and young ers worried that flying debris one day go through their lows."

r Millar's comments were e out by others we spoke to, weekend they had seen kards gather up a coping e and dump it in the middle of road. The policeman merely ed it to the side and left it. stone was all they lifted.

t the Tuck Shop, Mr Herbert y, fed up with the apparent tly, softly" approach of local e officers, said he felt obliged rganise a petition:

We, the undersigned, would to show our disapproval at lenient manner shown by the ce when called out to deal with people creating a public dis- r, fighting and using obscene uage on the night of Friday July and early Saturday ning 22nd July 1989 in Millar et, Crieff. This is becoming a lar occurrence on Friday and rday nights.

A copy of this petition will be to the Chief Constable in h, the local councillor and the l MP."

he Millar Street area is not e in disruption by drunks. As rted last week, the menace of ped, broken wine bottles left local open-air revellers is ing growing concern, and resi- s in the King Street/Commis-

ings). And James Square, of course, still sees more than its fair share of late-night activity.

We put the claims of a "softly- softly" policy to the police. Crieff's Inspector Lindsay Findlay denied it — in fact he looked at his incident book and noted the five arrests which were made in the town over the weekend. There were as many allegations of over- policing here as under-policing.

But he was concerned about Millar Street, which until now, he felt, had no special problem. He was aware of a disruption at the weekend — indeed he was investi- gating a case of serious assault but had no evidence it was a

out on the streets to be effective, after all. And weekends are always busy, if people do need police help the best thing to do is call Perth — they are in constant radio contact with the officers in the field."

They could be sent to any troubled area to defuse the situa- tion, and dispersing a crowd was "not the end of it" — monitoring did continue. As for arrests, they were dependent on witnesses to specific acts of public disorder. If the officers didn't actually see a crime committed, they needed those who did to come forward. "I can understand why sometimes

Cont. on page 3

wasn't long before an engineer was welding the gates around the Market Park . . .

Quietly, the travellers packed up and proceeded to move out of the town. They headed west.

At the same time, Tayside urged residents, community coun- cils and the local tourist associa- tion to withdraw their objections to the district council's plan for a permanent travelling folk site at the Highlandman.

As roads convener Cllr. Ray- mond Mennie put it: "I know they've forced a public enquiry but they could simply withdraw their objections the moment it gets under way. The travelling folk have to go somewhere and the regional council believe the district's choice at the Highland- man is very suitable.

Clearly they don't find the King Street area suitable, and they were erecting bollards and a heavy chain across the entrance.

"We don't want to harass the travellers, but the site is simply

EAGLESFIELD PLAN REFUSED

The controversial plan to develop a greenfield site at Eaglesfield Estate, Langside Drive, Comrie, has been refused.

The Perth developers, A. & J. Stephen Ltd., have been informed by Perth and Kinross that their proposal — even the re-designed one — was not acceptable.

There were four grounds for refusal:

The plan was contrary to the local development plan; it would mean over-development of the site and "unsatisfactory provision of private open space for in- dividual housing plots" and be detrimental to the residential amenities of future occupants; it would detract from the residential amenities presently enjoyed by the neighbours, and it would be detri- mental to the visual amenity of the area.

Local councillor Ewen Cameron said this week he thought the decision a wise one, but pointed out that the company had the right of appeal.

● Other plans, page 3.

HOMING IN ON CRIEFF FROM THE FOUR CORNERS

Families come, families go and families disperse to the four corners of the globe. But how often do three generations get together again in the old homestead?

It's over 50 years since the four Elder sisters of Crieff were with one another face to face, and they came from Canada, Zimbabwe, Northern Ireland and Bucking- hamshire to include four from Australia — for last weekend's family reunion on a grand scale.

Mrs Patricia Hurst, Mrs Dora Tucker, Mrs Janet Park and Mrs Hannah Robertson are the surviv- ing daughters of the Rev. Hugh Elder and Hannah Gilbert Mac- ainsh, who married in 1900. The family gathering took place at Knockearn, the former manse, now a boarding school of Morrison's Academy, with meals being served in the nearby Academy Hall.

"I'm even in the same bedroom I had as a girl," Mrs Tucker was pleased to find.

The family gathering was thought up two years ago by the sisters' niece, Mrs Alison Logie, when visiting her Canadian cous- ins.

"Everybody is getting on in- credibly well," she said on Sat- urday between a family golf tournament and team tennis com-

petition. "We're having a terrific time."

To keep everyone straight she compiled a 17-page dossier with the various family trees, photo- graphs, dormitory plans, duty list, emergency contingency plans, car- toons, a map and programme of events.

Despite all that, there was a minor panic when Mrs Hurst could not be found at lunchtime, day two. An over-efficient relative had locked her into Knockearn. "Having tried all the doors and windows, I remembered spare keys used to be kept in the kitchen and there was 'back door key' with a large label so I was able to let myself out," she joked.

From age 6 months to 86, every- one participated and there was a grand celebration dinner with speeches from each generation. It was followed by entertainment by family members, singing, dancing, piping, fiddling and comic sketches.

On Sunday the Macainsh graves were visited at Monzie Church be- fore the families dispersed, after lunch and fond farewells, to their far-flung homes.

Photo: Image Management.

Family Reunion Crieff 1989

Printed in Great Britain
by Amazon

37481616R00109